# Pessoa,
# The Metaphysical Courier

**Judith Balso**

Translated by Drew Burk

# Pessoa,
# The Metaphysical Courier

## Atropos Press

*Pessoa, Le Passeur Métaphysique* © 2006 by Judith Balso, translated as
*Pessoa, The Metaphysical Courier* by Drew Burk © 2011

ATROPOS PRESS
New York ● Dresden

US: 151 First Avenue # 14, New York, N.Y. 10003
Germany: Mockritzer Str. 6, D-01219 Dresden

cover design: Jason Wagner

ISBN #: 978-0-9831734-7-2

## *Translator's Note*

A book dealing with the philosophical nuances of the work of Judith Balso, Fernando Pessoa, and his heteronyms can be quite the challenge. I have re-translated all the excerpts of Pessoa's work as well as the other writers and philosophers mentioned in this book, and accept full responsibility for the perhaps difficult subtle changes and errors I made and hope the slight updating will allow for Pessoa and his heteronymous poetic accomplices to find another audience in this new century whose landscape doesn't seem that different than the one they describe at the turn of the last century.

I would first like to thank Judith Balso for her generous advice and counsel while translating this text. My thanks also go to Wolfgang Schirmacher for introducing me to the work of Fernando Pessoa and the extraordinary poetic philosophy of Judith Balso. I would also like to thank Sheridan Phillips, Hannes Charen, Jean-Christophe Plantin, Dan Hughes, L.E. Long, and the European Graduate School for their support and significant help during the long process of working on this project. And finally, I would like to thank Fernando Pessoa and his heteronyms for their contributions to poetry and philosophy.

# Contents

# 1

# The heteronymous emergence

Fernando Pessoa was born in Lisbon June 13, 1888 and died in Lisbon November 30, 1935: between these two dates, as the poet Caeiro states, his life belonged to him.

His artistic birth, his birth as a poet, is complex, and it develops over two periods. The first moment: March 1914, the apparition, as decisive as opaque, of the four heteronymous poets, Alberto Caeiro, Ricardo Reis, Álvaro de Campos, and Fernando Pessoa-himself. The second moment: the dramatic intellectual crisis of 1915-1916, during which the idea of the avant-garde and the meditation on the complexity and separation of metaphysics and art willingly battle and entangle themselves.

## Day of the heteronyms

Emerge as a poet, this was the injunction his friend, Mário de Sá-Carneiro, gave Pessoa in 1913: "Yes I am completely correct in saying what I have said to you ever since I met you: you should emerge as a poet." This meant, for Pessoa, emerging as four poets: the master Alberto Caeiro, Fernando Pessoa-himself, Ricardo Reis, and Álvaro de Campos. These are the distinct authors of four singular poetic oeuvres which he will much later name "heteronyms." But the apparition of these poets and their poems, that from then on offer themselves up as a constellation and separation, takes place prior to any thought that Pessoa has concerning what this group conveys or signifies. The poem initially shows itself through a multiple and problematic figure. To think what this singular poetic disposition thinks, to question and name this disposition, these are the tasks that immediately impose themselves upon the poet.

From this first birth, one obtains a narrative in which the striking precedence of the apparition of the heteronymy and its shock even to Pessoa are perceptible. Indeed, the poet provides a description of this in the now famous letter from January 13, 1935 to Adolfo Casais Monteiro, himself a poet, who amicably questioned Pessoa some twenty years after the event. It is necessary to cite and comment on this letter in its integrality, since it is a major document on heteronymy and its genesis (our submittal of evidence comes by way of the typography of these different parts and names):

- Around 1912, if I am not mistaken (and if I were, it would not be by much), the idea came to me to write some poems in a pagan manner. I sketched out certain things in an irregular style (not in the style of Álvaro de Campos but in a style which was semi-consistent), then I scrapped it. However, in this Indefinite shadowy light, a vague portrait of the person who was in the middle of creating it was sketched. (Without me knowing it, RICARDO REIS was born.)

- One and a half or two years later, I had the idea one day to pull a prank on Sá-Carneiro – to invent a bucolic poet, of a complicated species, and to present him to Sá-Carneiro, I no longer remember how, as a kind of reality. I spent several days trying to sketch out the poet without success. One day, when I had finally decided to give up, it was March 8, 1914 – I stepped away from a tall desk and grabbing some paper, I began to write, standing up, as I like to do when I can. And I wrote thirty some odd poems in a row in a sort of ecstasy that I couldn't explain. It was the most triumphant day of my life, and I would never know another day like it. I began with a title, "The Keeper of Sheep", and what followed was the emergence in me of someone who I immediately gave the name of Alberto Caeiro. Please excuse the absurdity of this phrase: my master appeared in me. This was the immediate sensation that I had.

- To such a degree that barely had I written these thirty some odd poems, I took another paper and I wrote, in a row as well, the six poems which make up the "Oblique Rain" of Fernando Pessoa. Immediately and in their entirety…it was the return of Fernando Pessoa-Alberto Caeiro to Fernando Pessoa, alone. Or better, it was the reaction of Fernando Pessoa against his non-existence as Alberto Caeiro.

- So it was that Alberto Caeiro appeared: I instinctively and subconsciously forced myself to discover disciples for him. I tore from his faux-paganism the latent Ricardo Reis: I found a name fitted for his size, because from that moment, I already saw him.

- And all of a sudden, according to a completely opposite derivation than that of Ricardo Reis, a new individual impetuously sprang fourth. From a spurt, and at the typewriter, without interruption or correction, the "Ode of Triumph" of Álvaro de Campos emerged – the "Ode" with this title and the man with the name that is his.

- So it was that I created an inexistent COTERIE. I placed all of this in the clay molds of reality. I regulated the influences, knew the friendships, heard in myself the discussions and the divergences of opinions, and in all of this, it seemed that I, who was the creator of all this, was the least present. *It seemed that it all took place independently of me.* And it still seems that way. If one day I could publish the aesthetic discussion between Ricardo Reis and Álvaro de Campos, you would see how different they are from one another and to what degree I have nothing to do with the whole affair.

Several things deserve to be underlined in this surprising story. The first thing is the fact that, in the heteronymy, the apparition of the poems of Caeiro comes first. This poet appears under the sign of abundance (thirty some odd poems are written quickly thereafter); he appears as a figure of mastery, which includes even his view concerning his creator. In the end, his existence can be deduced from a title, *The Keeper of Sheep* – which will remain the title of the principle work of Caeiro, and a proper noun.

It appears just as essential to take into account the initial disentanglement between the master and the one who will be identified as the orthonym[1]: far from pre-existing Caeiro or preceding him, Fernando Pessoa–"himself" owes his birth to Caeiro. Eclipsed by the eruption of the latter, he oscillates somewhat like a rhythm between the existence of Caeiro, whom alone authorizes in his manner the other to be a poet, and the disclaimer that the poem of the Keeper inflicts upon his own poetry. His apparition is thus second. That his fate from then on is to "not exist" when Caeiro appears deeply singularizes him amongst the heteronyms.

---

[1] The use of the word "orthonym", similar to a synonym in its etymology, refers, for Pessoa, to the same person, but in bearing another name carries within it a difference. This self-sameness of the "orthonym" is essential to understanding Pessoa's oeuvre and his use of the heteronym.

In other respects, we get the feeling that the orthonym interrupts the linear deployment of the heteronyms.

The engendering process of Ricardo Reis differs from that which gives birth to the three others. In his case, the name and the figure of the poet precede the poems. His strangeness indeed comes from the fact that he first appears as a fictional personality and, moreover, much earlier than the other heteronyms. The existence of the other poets clarifies the character of Reis, yet he nonetheless produces no poems whatsoever during this day of the heteronyms. Without a doubt, we should detect this peculiarity of the "reactive" character of Reis: at the heart of the *quartet*, he is the critic of the three others, not merely by taking harsh points of view vis-à-vis their respective poetries, but via the material itself of his own poetry, which he conceives as a poetry of the Idea. Ricardo Reis is what we could call a "differed disciple" of Caeiro: he first emerged in the form of an aesthetic program to which no oeuvre corresponds, because its materialization comes from the existence of the three other poets or, more specifically, from that of Campos, the modernist. Campos, against the aesthetic of Reis, will deploy an ample affirmative opposition.

This last disciple is a very liberal figure. Different from Pessoa or Reis, he derives from Caeiro an extreme latitude of being and, from the outset, has the strength of engaging an absolutely singular work. The use of a typewriter pleasantly places the material accent of modernity upon him. This Campos possesses a considerable initial energy which he will use up slowly in rubbing up against and making contact with the work of the master, as if his movement were to exhaust himself via the progressive knowledge he acquires from the impasses or aporias of his own project.

What emerges March 8, 1914 is thus a problematic multiplicity, a complex and splintered figure of the poem launching a debate, within the interior of poetry, which will prove to bear on poetry and poetry as thought.

## Poetic carbon dating

The successive terms through which Pessoa strives towards the heteronymous invention are obviously very important. How does he understand himself and think the existence of the heteronymy? It is extremely significant to know, for example, when the word "heteronymy", a word constructed by Pessoa, first appeared. When did these categories, "heteronymy" and "orthonymy", to which we have become accustomed and imagining them consubstantial to the oeuvre, originate? At what point did Pessoa place himself within these names? And what is, according to him, the clarification represented for giving such names to this configuration?

We are indeed led astray by a retroactive illusion: we use these names as if they were contemporaneous with the birth of the four poets, whereas their appearance comes infinitely much later. We must not forget that from 1914 to 1930, the heteronymous work published by Pessoa was not done in an organized, collected manner, but in a scattered order, according to the demands, authorities, and conjunctures that appeared to him. So it was that the poems of Campos largely preceded in their published existence those of the

Keeper and of Reis. Then, in the 1930s, Pessoa examined the idea of publishing the four heteronyms together and envisioned this as a way of maintaining the anonymity of the author. Several outlines exist of such a project under the title *Fictions of the Interlude*, which would have regrouped the four poets and included "A family discussion", a fictional polemical debate between Campos, Reis, Pessoa, Caeiro, and a certain António Mora – who would play the role of philosopher amongst poets. According to the documents that we have today, it seems that Pessoa orientated himself towards a presentation where the four heteronyms would have been maintained, but also his proper name as well. In this manner, he undertook a work of classification, probably definitively lost since the first editors to take possession of his files, Luís de Montalvor and João Gaspar Simões, untangled the arrangement without leaving a trace of it.

Throughout all the research, nothing indicates that the word heteronym appears before 1928. Indeed, it seems that the Bibliographical table, published in 1928 in the revue *Presença*, is the first text to propose the word and a definition; all the other essential documents were written between 1928 and 1935. The study dedicated to the orthonym will show the enormous impact of this point. Already we can see within the analysis of these dates and temporal disruptions the measurement of time needed for Pessoa to identify and name what was at stake in the heteronymous event.

However, it is very early on that he apprehends the decisive importance of what he had written, beginning on that date in March 1914, under the names of the poetic heteronyms. The profound intellectual crisis that he almost immediately traverses after the birth of these poets indeed finds its entanglement in the election of these works against the ensemble of what he had undertaken, in a much more infinitely public and spectacular form, under the successive signs of *paúlismo*, intersectionism, and sensationism. At the limit of the tormented sequence that opens up the project and reunites him with Sá-Carneiro, in order to create an avant-garde literary movement, the poet opts for the heteronymous oeuvre. And in this choice, his second birth as a poet plays itself out. Because different conceptions of poetry and art collide in and around the poet during 1915-1916, these were terrible years for him: enduring the war – the collapse and degradation from which it is made and to which Campos violently bears witness in the *Ultimatum*: the anxiety of going crazy and the temptation of letting himself be taken in by the doctrines of the theosophists. And he also must support his friend Sá-Carneiro, in flight to Paris, where suicide will find him.

Pessoa and Sá-Carneiro are 28 and 26 years old, respectively. The birth of the heteronyms provides to the former enough encouragement to form in 1915 with his friend and several others, the revue, *Orfeu*, Orpheus. This will open a tumultuous period of diverse scandals and, for Pessoa, great intellectual and subjective unrest.

December 6, 1915, uncompleted letter to Sá-Carneiro:

> Psychically, I am surrounded. [...] I am in a disarray and intellectual anguish that you imagine poorly. [...] I am haunted by the idea that the truth is perhaps really there, in

Theosophy. Do not think that I have slipped into madness; I do not believe this. I am dealing with a grave crisis of a mind which *fortunately* takes something from these crises. [...] It is the horror and the attraction of the co-existing abyss in the hereafter of the soul. A metaphysical fear my dear Sá-Carneiro!

## March 14, 1916 from Pessoa to Sá-Carneiro:

I am in one of those days *where I never had a future*. There is only the immobile present, with a wall of anxiety all around. [...] There is also the state of war with Germany, but the pain caused suffering much before this.

It is in this state of torment that Pessoa comes across the idea of movements in art. The heteronymous oeuvre for him at this time is still nothing but a given amongst others: he treats it as a reserve, a kind of hidden treasure from which he withdraws several pieces, several ammunitions, several combustibles which are enough to provoke explosions, noises, and fireworks. Like a magician he pulls from his hat three poems from Campos ("Opium Eater", "Ode of Triumph", "Maritime Ode") and several works from the orthonym ("The Sailor", "Oblique Rain"). However, neither the master Caeiro, nor Reis, will as yet be known to this public: they will respectively wait till the years 1925 and 1924 for a part of their work to be published. These choices are the result of the explicit will to act in art, and to act in art by "movements". In such a moment, Campos is the central figure, as much by his poems, as by his loud interventions in the press, or by his provocative prose in which *Ultimatum* is the prized piece. Campos is the man of circumstance, the spokesperson for secret heteronymy. He is the one who works out a meeting ground with the European literary and artistic avant-gardes and who integrates their materials. But he is also the one who announces their separation.

The *Ultimatum* against the war of 1914-1918 (published by Campos in 1917 in the revue *Portugal futurista*) will be Pessoa's extreme entry point into the avant-garde project. Whereas it is striking to note that despite formally futuristic aspects, *Ultimatum* is violent, provocative, constantly insulting for all authority whether state or intellectual – this text distances itself from futurism in all its references. In philosophy, a hatred of Henri Bergson, who, on the contrary, was a veritable object of a futurist cult; disdain and contempt for all types of "isms" and the loud and hollow European idols; condemnation and critical of the same war to which F. T. Marinetti professed to extol and adore like a new god: point by point, profound divergences declared themselves under the appearance of a maximum conjunction.

For Pessoa, the poem is a freedom to do away with the object and a freedom to invent new images which are no longer "images of" something, but artificial constructions no less perfectly real in their own right. Rendering possible that art was no longer illusionist, but "lucid" – re-iterating one of Campos' favorite epithets – and that art was no longer so much this fiction conscious of being a fiction (in which at least an entire part of modern art, having barely been born, will lose itself) but a fiction conscious in its own manner of being real, exactly as machines or bridges are real. The importance within this poetic framework accorded to the city and the machine is more profound than the futurists had thought: the machine in particular incarnates a "non-object", a latent model of the real as an abstract construction. It is in this manner the emblem of what art thinks and affirms of itself from then on.

Paradoxically, this new vision of art will drive Pessoa to abandoning, almost at the exact moment he is creating *Orfeu*, the project of constructing a literary avant-garde movement. So it is that the decision of withdrawing himself from this scene is announced in a letter to Armando Cortez Rodriguez from January 19, 1915, three months before the first issue of the revue:

> To act upon humanity, to contribute by all my efforts to civilization, this is what has become the grave, smashing objective of my life. More and more art seems to be the most important and the most terrible mission – a duty to accomplish with ardor, with a monastic austerity, eyes focused on the creative stakes of civilization of the entire oeuvre of art. [...] I am returning to myself. During several years, I traveled in order to gather ways of feeling. Now, I have seen and felt everything, I have the duty of closing myself up into my mind and to work as much as I can, and in every area where I can, in order to help civilization progress and in order to enlarge the conscious of humanity. [...] What I call insincere are things made in order to surprise as well as those things, *note this well, it is important* – which do not contain a fundamental metaphysical idea – which is to say, those things in which one does not even find a small breath of the gravity and mystery of Life.

> I do not need to explain to you how much this attitude [...] led to the birth of a deaf incompatibility with those who surround me. We are not talking about a violent incompatibility, but an impatience concerning all those who assign inferior goals to art, and who are artists as if they are playing in order to

distract themselves, or like arranging a living room in a tasteful manner – this is a genre of art which illustrates quite well what I mean, because it does not go Beyond this, and has no other goal, if I may express myself accordingly, than being *decoratively* artistic. It is from here that my entire "crisis" arises. Fortunately, it is not a crisis that I have to complain about.

The preoccupation is already no longer to act upon art or within art, but indeed to act upon humanity.

The last vestige of influence from the others on my character has disappeared (*he writes again in a "autobiographical fragment" from November 21, 1914*). I have understood – in feeling that I could and I was going to dominate the intense and infantile desire to "start Intersectionism" – that I was from then on in the tranquil possession of myself.

A light illuminated me with lucidity. I am born.

The journey and then abandonment of the avant-garde movements in art: such are the conditions for the "second birth" of Pessoa as poet. He makes lateral use of the avant-garde: he provided it with his brilliance, not the other way around. And when he renounced it, it was explicitly for another path in art in order to return to the heteronymy that would deliberately distance the poem from art and, in doing so, make art out of being other.

# 2
# The enigma of the semi-heteronymy

At the moment of gathering up the works of Caeiro, Reis, Pessoa-orthonym, and Campos for publication, Bernardo Soares was rejected from *Fictions of the Interlude* by the motive that the author of *The Book of Disquiet* wrote only prose while "in the *Fictions* [...] verse was predominating." And what is more, Soares is in no way part of the birth of March 1914. The writing of the book is much more in line with the time, marked by an indecision which will never be reabsorbed: indeed, two non-unified strata co-exist in this work, one contemporary with the avant-gardes, the other an imprint of a mastery and singularity more manifestly leaning towards the heteronymous quartet. Accompanying this movement, the character of Bernardo Soares succeeds that of Vicente Guedes, the first incarnation of the character of *guarda-livros* – literally the bookkeeper, or the "keeper of the books" – who writes his own personal journal in the margins of his grand ledgers.

Soares is, however, re-incorporated with the heteronymy by Pessoa, in a milder form – that of the "semi-heteronymy".

What does this category, which is just as obscure and bizarre as "orthonym", denote?

## Poem and prose

Soares equally sees himself attributed by the poet the ambiguous status of "literary personality". Could the heteronymy be comprised of two halves: literary personality on one side, literary production on the other – the semi-heteronymy being the one reduced to the first component? It is difficult to imagine just what a "literary personality" separated from the production written under his name could very well be. This division appears to convey the figure of the writer as *deus ex machina* pulling the strings of literary process. Should we consider Soares simply as a straw man of Pessoa, to make him the fictional author of the book in which the true "personality" of the poet expresses itself? That would be equal to cramming semi-heteronymy onto pseudonymy.

Another approach is possible, sketched out by Pessoa himself, which consists in thinking of prose as presenting an obstacle to heteronymy. It would offer up a particular resistance to literary depersonalization and would render the elaboration of a separate work aleatory: "In prose, it is more difficult to make oneself other", Pessoa notes regarding *The Book of Disquiet*. Eduardo Lourenço deduced from this remark that Pessoa found himself in this work "less distant from his profound speech than [in] all poetry."

Would the semi-heteronymy not then, on the contrary, be the product of the part of his prose that constantly clings to the edge of the poem: Soares being part heteronym in this case, because he is part poet?

This hypothesis at first glance can appear to be paradoxical because Soares, author of a very small number of deceptive poems, is above all a prodigious writer of prose. His art, unique to Portuguese poetry, shatters the organization, capacities, sonorities, and rhythm of the language, like the prose of the *Confessions* or, more still, like that found in *Rêveries* did for the French language. There is a before and after Soares in Portuguese prose, in the sense that there was a before and after Rousseau.

The semi-heteronym moreover starts out convinced of the intrinsic superiority of prose. Not only does Soares write: "Nothing that life can bring or take away from me makes me weep. Certain pages in prose, however, have made me cry", he does not hesitate in declaring that "prose encompasses the entirety of art" because "language contains the entire world" and prose is the "complete freedom of speech" in which are contained "all possibilities of saying and thinking." In opposition to this freedom of prose, verse, even when it is irregular, obeys rhythmic laws which are so much restrictions and coercions of "automatic apparatuses of oppression and sanction." Prose, on the contrary, loosens up language because it dispenses with form to which all other arts, and above all poetry, are beholden. Thus, it would be definitively superior or supreme by a capacity of "indirect equivalence" that Soares names "transposition". By this word, Soares, this writer of prose, finds himself in the company of Mallarmé who thought that Music, for example, proposed nothing that could not be rendered "with an equal magnificence – moreover for our consciousness, this clarity – [by] the ancient and holy elocution". For Soares, there is always something, "childish, mnemonic, auxiliary, and initial" about the poem, and poetry constitutes at best a sort of propaedeutic of prose used by children. For him, prose does not take second place, a position from which it would immediately falter if we grant him the idea that it should be a position of origin, and that the poem, in a sense, would be purified prose: "Rose out of prose", to prolong a beautiful word play by Philippe Beck in *D'un fumier sans pourquoi*.

The prose of the semi-heteronym is what Baudelaire called for as a poem in prose. The Portuguese language seems to have mysteriously been chosen to accomplish the program which the French poet sketched out in the "Letter to Arsène Houssaye": "Who has not dreamed […] the miracle of a poetic prose, musical without rime or rhythm, sufficiently supple and erratic in order to adapt itself to the lyrical movements of the soul, to the oscillations of reverie, to the shocks of consciousness?" Such lines seem to describe in advance *The Book of Disquiet*, to the point that every reader will dream of Soares' Lisbon within the inspiration of the following lines: "It is above all the visiting of enormous cities; it is from the intersection of their innumerable relations which gives birth to this obsessive ideal." Does Soares not write: "I judge myself poet of my prose, within the winged moment it was born in me"? So it is that he declares himself poet of his prose, there where Caeiro, for his part, displays the prose of his verse. What does this fingerprint of the poem imprint onto the prose of the semi-heteronymy?

## What does the dreamer "see"?

*The Book of Disquiet* is inhabited by a dreamer, sometimes a wanderer, almost always solitary, most often holed up in an office where he exercises his work as an accountant's assistant, or pressed up against his window high up in his room under the rooftops in the lower neighborhoods of Lisbon. The law of the book is that of emergence, necessarily deprived of order, and of the visions of this dreamer. What the publisher of the book calls "fragments" each begin being concerned with a vision and are only complete once the thought of this held vision exhausts itself. Why speak of vision and dreamer? These words, which belong to *The Book of Disquiet*, play an essential role: the first word differentiates the eye of Soares from the "sunflower gaze" of the Keeper; the second represents the unique and eminent task recognized by the tiny employee who writes this prose. "The vision of the dreamer is not like that of someone who sees things," it is said in this book. For Soares, "the only thing that is important is what the dreamer sees" – elsewhere he continues, "my vision of things always suppresses within itself what my reverie cannot use."

The suggestion of this word "reverie", which I use in order to translate throughout *The Book of Disquiet*, the Portuguese word *sonho*, has been much deliberated, because this so-called state is not linked to sleep. Antonio Tabucchi, in his Postface to the Bourgois edition (1988), thought it possible to extrapolate an insomnia from this book. To dream is deliberately supported by Soares as a configuration other than consciousness, as an "in-between" conducive to the grasping of things in the mystery of their existence.

Soares underlines that his "immediate instinct" is to apply an attention which is "absent-mindedly acute to certain details of the Exterior" in order to capture what comes from the being of things. This singular exercise, which is all his own, is to "abstract whatever there is dreamable (*rêvable*) from each object or event by leaving for dead within the exterior world all that is real." This category, the real, negatively defined by Soares as the "non-dreamable" – emerges in him with a particular force. The power peculiar to reverie is to distinguish within the thing its dreamable being and its opaque reality. The being of things is also what Soares names "the true reality", in opposition to the reality of their existence. The dreamer thus recognizes the distinctions that he establishes: "The true reality of an object is barely a part of it; all the rest is the cumbersome payment that it accords to matter in exchange for its existence in space." Symmetrically, "there is no reality in space for certain phenomena which in reverie have a palpable reality."

Soares follows the traces of Gérard de Nerval from *Aurélia*: "Ah, how many times have my reveries themselves rose up within me as things", he writes "not in order to substitute themselves in me for reality, but in order to make me confess that they are equals, in that they do not appear from my will, but from the outside, like that tram that appears at the corner of the street…" He welcomes, without sorting it out, all that comes from reverie, all that proves capable of floating within it: its decantation is unconscious and involuntary.

His reverie, however, is not an operation of derealization. On the contrary, it presents itself as an equal to reality to the extent that it springs forth from an identical exteriority as reality. It is in this manner that it is capable of not capturing our phantasmagorias, but the being itself of things. This affirmation allows Soares to refute the accusation of idealism. He is inclined to use the term "realist", which he justifies as such: "If it were not for my manner of always dreaming, of living in a perpetual estrangement, I could, in good faith, classify myself as a realist, which is to say, an individual for whom the exterior world is an independent nation." "But", he adds, "I prefer to not give myself a name, in order to be what I am with a certain obscurity." His only profession of faith is this: "To dream is always a sort of duty that I have." This idea of an outstanding duty for Soares positions him at the antipodes of the figure of the dilettante or the amateur. As Eduardo Lourenço finally notes, dreaming is his specialization: "I am not a dreamer", Soares insists, "I am exclusively a dreamer."

This reverie is destined to create a site opposed to all deceptive locations of consciousness. Soares refuses any ontological capacity of clear and distinct thought in order to disseminate it within reverie. Which is to say, the metaphysical allocation of this activity materializes a ferociously anti-Cartesian method: "to pull out of the undecidable and obscure is something I experience as universal disasters and cataclysms."

## The dream machine

"I don't think it to be either a human or literary error", Soares writes, "to attribute a soul to things we call inanimate. *To be a thing, is to be objectified by an attribution.*" This affirmation gives way to numerous ulterior developments: each thing possesses its own particular expression which comes from the outside, and the "environment (*milieu ambiant*) is the soul of things." In the end, it gives way to this synthetic "definition" of the thing: "Each thing results from the interaction of three axes, and these three axes which construct it: a certain quantity of material, the way in which we interpret it, and the milieu where it is located."

Reverie, in which the being of things comes clean, professes itself, is inseparable from the work of prose. Soares takes care to meticulously highlight this link: "The one who knows how to write is the one who knows how to see his reveries clearly, or who knows how to see life through reverie, to see life immaterially, in photographing it with the dream machine." Reverie thus demands from prose a work of precision whose stake is crucial. To be capable of "saying a thing, is to conserve the virtue from it and to take away the terror." Things contain terror and virtue, and because of this, they are susceptible to creating a terrifying metaphysical anxiety. The poem, contrary to the semi-heteronymous prose, is not a "dream machine", and does not do away with terror nor capture the virtue which emanates from things. The semi-heteronymous prose alone is capable of this.

But in order for it to do this, it must be capable of "speak[ing] in an absolute manner, photographically, outside the norm and outside of the everyday." The pride of Soares is to be able to affirm: "*I will not have spoken: I will have said.*" The most developed example of a prose with such a capacity resides in the possibility of literally naming the being of existence. Here it is, in its complex face-off with grammar, which is difficult to render completely in English:

> If I wanted to say I exist, I would say: I am (Sou). If I wanted to say I exist as an individualized soul, I would say : I am myself (Sou eu). But if I wanted to say I exist as an entity which directs and forms itself, and which exerts in the most direct fashion the divine function of creating itself, how do I then use the word "Being" without immediately turning it into a transitive verb? Then, triumphantly and antigramatically promoted as supreme being, I shall say: I myself am (Sou-me). I will have explained a complete philosophy in three words. Can we ask more from philosophy and verbal expression?

We discover within these lines how the prose of the anonymous employee strives to ontologically rival philosophy. It is a singular monster: a non-philosophical ontological prose.

### Writing at the level of vision

To pass from the simple word to the telling of prose is, according to Soares, to cross over into "making" (*faire*). The prose sentence in Soares' work has a power of a making (*un faire*) from which he expects in particular the re-absorption of the mystery of the existence of things.

This imperative of the sentence as a "telling" (*dire*) accentuates the fragmentary state of the text which can first be inferred from the scattered visions of the dreamer. The incompletion of the book in no way can be constituted as an extrinsic trait. It is not the effect of indecision (*velléitarisme*) of the one writing, nor the consequence of an interruption of its organization because of death, but it is also not the result of the impossibility of fastening together disparate pieces of text. It is in an essential manner that this book exists in a fractured mode: It can only develop within a multiplication without order, without connections with its parts. Each "fragment" possesses a law of composition particular to itself. Each "fragment" is either complete in itself or incomplete and, in all cases, self-contained in being a prose poem. Can we really name something a "fragment" that possesses such a perfect internal unity? What gives existence to this book is nothing other than the occurrences that the reverie directs and prescribes. Thus, it welcomes variants and amendments at the same time it is open to the most extreme gaps.

Because reverie is born without laws, it goes along capturing the changing and updating expressivity of things. The things of the city with its houses, windows, rooftops, the passersby, the tram, the chiming of the town bell, the grocery clerk, the fruit stand, the on-duty policeman, the light, the hands of rain on the window, the reflection of the moon, the variations of the estuary, the infinite mobility of the clouds...Soares declares to not dare write "more than pieces, chunks, inscriptions of the non-existent" precisely because the existence of things is uncertain, fleeting, and transitory. Sometimes they already no longer exist by the time the hand finishes writing them down. A vision "fades away the moment we possess it." It is "an interval between nothing and nothing." Soares describes his book as a "patchwork (*crochet*) of things, an interval...nothing." He considers it both haphazard and carefully meditated like woven impressions without succession and which are nonetheless coherent. Neither a collection of sparse fragments – is a collection of poems made of fragments? – nor incomplete, it is, in its very principle itself, unachievable. It is not the preliminary sketch of a project, which is incapable of being achieved, nor the abandoned construction site of another book. It is what it must be, within the disorder where it was born, without any order being superimposed onto it, not even from the hand of the one who writes it.

At the end of the day, the lone true incoherence of the book is internal: it is the permanent visible traces of two successive periods within the ontological figure of the dreamer, initially under the symbolist and romantic influences, and later contemporaneous with the heteronymous adventure. As for this flaw of unity, Pessoa had as project the hope of "adapting the oldest pieces, which do not correspond with the psychology of Bernardo Soares, as it now appears", and he also dreamt of undertaking a general revision of style, prior to publication. He died however before having the chance. In regards to this singular point, it is true that death won.

## What is *tedio*?

It is possible that things resist reverie, refusing to enter into it. The mystery of their existence thus invades the world and from this mystery oozes a horror without name. "A sea separated from living things which have [become] foreign," the exterior world begins to exist in such moments under the frightened eyes of the dreamer "like an actor on stage: he is there, but he is something else." Things lose their expressivity, shying away from any identification and no longer offering any foothold on reverie; they are filled up in some way by the void and die: "Everything is emptier than the void. Everything can be reduced to the chaos of inexistent things. Reflecting on all of this, if I look around me [...] what I see are houses without expression, faces without expression, gestures without expression. Stones, bodies, ideas – all of this is dead. Nothing tells me anything. Nothing is known to me, not that I find it bizarre, but because I don't know what it is. I have lost the world."

When things cease to be expressive, not only does the world become mysterious, but opaque and impossible to grasp. This undecipherable and insignificant exterior tissue maddens the thought of the dreamer. Soares gives to this state the name *tedio*. Neither malaise, nor mind numbing, nor tiring, it includes all of these without resembling them. It is the "physical sensation of chaos, and that chaos is everything." The *tedio* is a

> feeling of desolation without a precise location, of the wreckage of the entire soul. I feel that I have lost a complacent God, that the Substance of all things is, from now on, dead. And the universe of sensation for me is a cadaver which I liked when it was life, but everything transformed into nothing in the still warm light of the last colored and reflecting clouds. My *tedio* takes on the allures of horror; my lassitude is fear.

The bigger the *tedio*, the more sovereign the horror of being alive: "I know neither who I am nor what I am. I lie here – like I am surrounded by a crumbling wall which has broken up on top of me, under the sudden collapsed nothingness of the entire universe."

It is impossible to give to this terrible metaphysical state the feeble name of "boredom", which would translate it to the letter. Rather we would think of the Sartrean test of "nausea". But the best solution, without doubt, is to keep and impose the Portuguese name, which, in the end, identifies the singularity of this terror before an exhausted world overwhelmed in the brutal loss of expressivity. In the same way the word "spleen"[2] had to be re-introduced and then conserved in order to designate a certain modern melancholy and existential disenchantment. Moreover, Soares sometimes uses the word *tedio* in Portuguese as if it were a proper noun. He talks of a feeling "worse than *tedio* but to which no other word than *tedio* suffices." All the variants of *tedio* are metaphysical: *tedio* "of the constantly new"; *tedio* of "discovering under the false diversity of things, the continual identity of everything"; or still *tedio* of perceiving that "in all of this – sky, earth, world – there is nothing else, nothing else in all this but me."

## A metaphysical ledger

One effect of *tedio* is the stagnation of everything: a complete suspension of will, of emotion, thought, and finally writing itself. This is when the anxious desire of "sleeping through life" installs itself in order to exterminate

---

[2] See the translation of Charles Baudelaire's great work, *Paris Spleen: little poems in prose*. Translated by Keith Waldrop, Wesleyan, 2009

*tedio*, handing it over to sleep within the horror of the perception of chaos in which the universe resides and that spills out over everything: "To sleep! To lie down! To be abstractly conscious of breathing tranquilly, without a world, without stars, without a soul, a dead sea of emotions reflecting the absence of stars!"

Intervening in the brevity and precarity of the visions of the dreamer, *tedio* is another intrinsic cause of the interruptions accentuated within the writing of the book. Soares affirms having pushed forward as much as possible his notations on the state in which *tedio* plunges itself, the place where the growing horror and malaise are obstacles to the act of writing itself. The character of the book's *trechos* (fragments) merges with the brutal collapsing of thought and the incessant passages of reverie towards *tedio* and from *tedio* to complete paralysis, to stagnation. *The Book of Disquiet* records these victories and defeats of the dreamer over the mysteries of things and strangeness of the exterior world.

A number of times, Soares depicts himself as writing in the margins of great ledgers, which he uses by profession, passing from the notation of numbers to his fictive activity of noting in prose his activity as dreamer. Which is to say: *The Book of Disquiet* is a metaphysical ledger in which active and passive accounts succeed each other by chance without the bottom line ever being determined – nor could it be. Thus, it would be pure vanity to try to arrange in some logical order this correspondence, or as Soares sometimes calls it, this "biography without facts", which has neither recipient nor dates. This notebook of notations, as fugitive as what it notes, sketched out as much from thought as from its impotence, is undertaken by someone who writes like painters paint: all the time.

Because it is made up of notations which are unarticulated between themselves, the book of Soares could be presented as the inaugural and personal laboratory of the whole oeuvre. Could this book be the secret source of the poems?

Sparse elements in the book indicate intriguing and striking similarities. So it is that a tone of homogeneity is perceptible between certain fragments of the book and the deliberately romantic sequences of the grand poems of Campos: the same posted "decadentism", the same hostility towards humanitarianism, the same ontological egalitarianism. Like the orthonym, Soares explores the divisions of consciousness, rejects the dialectical figure, shows a quasi-nihilist skepticism. Caeiro is often taken apart by him, his thought criticized, but the book refers also in certain places to the conceptions of the Keeper; for example, the particular limit that each thing has and the ever new identity of each viewed thing. As for the lines that follow, they correspond with the Lucretian fatalism of the most beautiful verse of Reis: "Equal is the abstract destiny of man and things – an equally mysterious indifference within the algebra of mystery."

If in semi-heteronymy it is more difficult to make oneself other, it is also more difficult to make oneself other than the heteronymous poets. Thus, it sometimes seems that we come across in *The Book of Disquiet* the program or sketch of a poem that we recognize precisely by the fact that it has been written. The examination of reciprocal dates is rarely possible, because most of the fragments of the book cannot be dated with certitude. It would seem, however, that we are dealing rather with notations after the fact, of revisits to the poem by the prose.

Such is the case, for example, with a fragment dated December 1, 1931 that strongly evokes "Tobacco Shop", a poem written in 1928. Elsewhere, the fragment titled "Sentimental Education" reverberates with the sadomasochistic construction of the "Maritime Ode", "Millimetres" with poem 40 from *The Keeper of Sheep*. At the same time, the visions of the dreamer, the malediction of *tedio*, the innate power of the *desassossego* singularizes this prose enough for us to absolutely distinguish it from the poetic heteronymy and, by consequence, we do away with the idea that these poems are reducible to the sketch of the poems they closely resemble. The "repetition" in prose each time introduces an ontological shift or displacement upon which the book seems to meditate and put into practice. Take for example the passage in which Soares cites, in praise, the poem of Caeiro to the glory of his "village". The Keeper upholds the following paradox:

> [...] I have the dimensions of what I see
> And not the size which belongs to me.

Commenting on these two lines from the Keeper, Soares writes:

> Sentences like these which seem to grow all by themselves, without being dictated by any specific will, *wash me clean of all the metaphysics that I spontaneously add to life.* After having read them, I go to my window, whose view is of a narrow street, I look at the vast sky and its numerous stars,

and I feel free, carried by a winged splendor whose vibration I feel throughout my entire body. [...]

From then on, *conscious of having understood how to see, I contemplate the vast objective metaphysics of the infinite skies*, with an assurance which makes me want to die in singing. "I have the dimensions of what I see!" And the vague lunar clarity, which is totally my own, from its indecisive gleam, begins to damage the blue-black of the horizon. [...] But I return to myself and I calm myself down. "I have the dimensions of what I see!" And this sentence becomes my entire soul, I rely on all my emotions, and all of a sudden, the indecipherable peace of a brilliant moonlight stretches out into nightfall and descends upon me, inside, like upon the city – outside.

Caeiro here practices his own mastery of the semi-heteronym, that of the master hostile to metaphysics, the master of "seeing". But the precariousness of this anti-metaphysical influence of the poet on the writer of prose is delicate. The conversion to "seeing" remains tributary, in the prose, from the physical state of things, from the unstable disposition of moonlight and the night. Soares, without any difficulty, will agree with Caeiro that "things have no meaning, they have an existence"; but it is via existence itself that Soares is encountered. His prose does not completely part from metaphysics because it needs to be an interpretation of existence.

## The Disquieter

Soares writes what he sometimes calls, thinking of course of Rousseau, his "Confessions", but the character has neither a date of birth, nor birthplace, and his autobiography lacks all the "facts", his history all "life": "And me, that which is really me, I am the center of all of this, a center which does not exist, if only by a geometry of the abyss; I am this nothing around which this movement turns, without any other goal than to turn, and without existing by itself, except by the reason that every circle possesses a center. Me, that which is really me, I am the well without an inside, but with the viscosity of wells, the center of everything with nothing around it." Soares also describes himself as "the abstract center of impersonal sensations, a fallen sensitive mirror towards the variety of the world". At the heart of the semi-heteronymy, as with the heteronymy, only the void exists.

*The Book of Disquiet* records different moments of the battle of a thought grappling with the will of mastering the inherent mystery of the existence of things and the world: "There is no other problem than that of reality, and that one, is indeed unsolvable and alive – what do I know of the difference between a tree and a reverie?"

The greatness of this book is neither the reverie nor even the *tedio*, but the incessant transit from one to the other. The identity of the dreamer finds itself threatened as soon as he attributes too big a place to reverie. Because this is the equivalent of "giving an excessive importance to something which separated itself from us, which rose up and manifested itself, as much as possible, as reality, losing at the same time, any right to our nuanced attention." Reverie in this case can, in a way, finds itself objectified: it becomes in its own manner a part of reality; it confuses itself with the things that it is supposed to capture and whose presence it must filter. To prevent it from being this way, Soares is obliged to firmly establish a distinction between reverie and the real: "The figures of reverie and those of the world – have an equal and proper but different reality." The habit of dreaming induces yet another difficulty for Soares, that of conceiving other consciousness than his own. One must also fight off the autism of the dreamer: "One of my constant preoccupations is to understand how it is that the others exist, how is it that there are souls that are not mine – consciousness foreign to my consciousness which, being conscious, seems to me as being unique."

These upheavals, these wanderings, these uncertainties make up the *desassossego* that gives its name to the title of the book. There is no better way to understand the word than through what Soares pens as the apparent contrary definition of the word, *sossego*:

> Nothing however pulls me toward the high despite the fact nothing no longer pulls me toward the low. I feel free as if I have ceased to exist and however I have become conscious of this. [...] I see without having the intention of seeing, and I see without remedy. I attentively participate within a non-existent spectacle. I do not feel the soul, but tranquility [*sossego*]. Exterior, clear, immobile things, even if they move, appear to me like they must have appeared to Christ, when from way on high, Satan came to tempt him. Things are nothing and I understand that Christ didn't allow himself to be tempted. They are nothing and what I don't understand is that Satan, having the knowledge of the ages, imagined it possible to tempt with so little.

In the state of *sossego*, things have stopped worrying thought, of showing themselves to be threatening to it. Things are at peace with thought: their existence no longer exhibits the mystery of existence. By an inverse coincidence with the "seeing" of Caeiro, things in this appeased vision of the dreamer are nothing more than their naked existence. Thus it is the *tedio*, not the *sossego*, which is the true opposite of *desassossego*. Armand Guibert proposed translating this word as an "interior stirring", but the *desassossego* more precisely expresses the metaphysical anxiety or worry particular to the dreamer. In this regard, the word "intranquility" appears weak. "Intranquility" has the strength and beauty of a neologism. But Soares is, very profoundly, a disquieter whose work site is not the poem but the obscure Rua dos Douradores in the heart of this Lisbon of the lower neighborhoods where this strange office worker pretends to live and work.

## The egalitarianism of prose

Why must the dreamer-metaphysician borrow his traits, habits, and profession from this anonymous man who, lacking all social and intellectual prestige, is Bernardo Soares? It is to the most ordinary and obscure of men whom he thus gives the task of enduring the state of disquiet that makes up this book, to use his life to untangle and to tangle up again the mystery of the existence of things and universes. According to Soares, humanity finds itself divided by an ontological bet which is consubstantial and eternal: "*There will always be a struggle in this world, without a decision or victory, between the one who likes that which is not because it exists and the one who likes that which is because it doesn't exist.*" This warning from the Disquieter calls for two remarks. The conflict in question is presented without a way out: there will never be neither a decision nor a victory. Second, the phrase deliberately inverts being and existence. There, where we expected existence, the "there is and there is not" of being appears. In the eyes of Soares, there thus exists two irreconcilable and incompatible ontological "positions". Two positions and two alone. Each of us either belongs to one or the other, even when we are not conscious of it. Each of us is capable of bringing a new piece to this "geography of our consciousness of ourselves" that *The Book of Disquiet* in its own way inaugurates. "We have never lived as much," Soares reminds us, against the temptation of living without affronting this figure, "than when we have thought a lot."

That the Disquieter has this character constitutes on the part of Pessoa a declaration about humanity, about its composition: "We others, in the shadow, lost amongst the minions and barbers," Soares writes, "we constitute humanity." What distinguishes him from a grocery clerk or from the tailor that he goes to is that he knows how to write. But, "in the soul," he insists, "I am their equal." This prose thus takes away a privilege from the poets in denying them the monopoly on metaphysical and ontological worry.

Witness this excerpt from *The Book of Disquiet*. The grand guidelines of the book are admirably concentrated here as well as the singularity of Soares' prose:

> Whoever has read the pages of this book will no doubt have concluded that I am a dreamer. And he will have concluded incorrectly. I lack the money to be a dreamer.

> Great melancholies and sorrows infused with tedium can only exist within an atmosphere of comfort and solemn luxury. That's why Poe's Egaeus, pathologically absorbed in thought for hours on end, lives in an ancient, ancestral castle where,

beyond the doors of the lifeless drawing room, invisible butlers administer the house and prepare the meals.

Great dreams demand special social circumstances. One day, when the doleful cadence of a certain passage I'd written made me excitedly think of Chateaubriand, it didn't take me long to remember that I'm not a viscount, nor even a Breton. On another occasion, when I'd written something whose content seemed to recall Rousseau, it likewise didn't take long for me to realize that, besides not being the noble lord of a castle, I also lack the privilege of being a wanderer from Switzerland.

But there is also the universe at the Rua dos Douradores. Here as elsewhere, God watches over us to make sure the enigma of existence knows no end. However poor my dreams may be, within the landscape of carts and crates from whose wheels and boards I tear away an image, they're what I have and am able to have.

The sunsets, no doubt, really exist somewhere else. But even from the fourth-floor room that looks out over the city, it's possible to contemplate infinity. An infinity with warehouses down below, it's true, but with stars up above...This is what occurs to me as I look out of my high window overlooking the street at the end of day, caught between the dissatisfaction of the bourgeois that I'm not, and the sadness of the poet that I will never be.

All the beauty of *The Book of Disquiet* can be found here: focused on the debate between thought and things, this prose which would prefer to render the poem destitute, constantly turns to the poem.

# 3

# A small memento from the heteronymous poetic oeuvre

**Alberto Caeiro** is the author of a volume that includes 49 poems under the title *The Keeper of Sheep*, as well as the six poems of the *Shepherd in Love*, and an ensemble called *Detached Poems*.

Caeiro is, from their own admission, the "master" of Campos and Reis. The totality of poems found within *The Keeper of Sheep* was not written in a single day. The 30 or so poems which we find within the primary manuscripts constituted the founding movement and would later be partially recomposed and completed in what we could designate as a small veritable treatise on poetry, metaphysics, and art.

*Detached Poems* appears at one moment as variations and another moment as left-over scraps. The poems add nothing fundamental to what was already expressed in the volume of the *Keeper*. Pessoa, on the contrary, was quite attached to the poems from *Shepherd in Love* which inscribe within the work of Caeiro the strangeness that he is capable of being in love – which highlights the non-rigidity of the Keeper's oeuvre, its flexibility and freedom, put to the test by love.

This fictitious life is dated by Pessoa as 1889-1915 – the birth of Caeiro is thus one year later than his own; Caeiro's death, at a precocious 26 years-old, is the same year as the death of Sá-Carneiro.

The fictitious dates from *The Keeper of Sheep* anticipate the time of the real writing: 1911-1912, instead of 1914. This can also be said for the texts from the *Shepherd in Love*, distributed during the years 1913-1915, while only two of the poems had been written in 1914 and the others between 1915 - 1920, and finally 1930.

The first poems of Caeiro published by Pessoa were in 1925, in the revue *Athena*. The first and matrixial within the heteronymy, this oeuvre will not have been a contemporary of the generation of *Orfeu*. Sá-Carneiro, moreover, complains to himself about the absence his friend takes in regards to Caeiro concerning their enterprise: "Even though I think it is correct, I must admit I regret that Caeiro doesn't adhere to *paúlismo*." Empirically, we could invoke the brutal ending of *Orfeu* after the second issue of the revue and the death of Sá-Carneiro, because, in one of the outlines created by Pessoa for the third issue, we can see the name of Caeiro was included. But, in the end, 10 years of silence will come between the emergence of the master's oeuvre and its publication. During this difficult time within the various avant-garde movements, the oeuvre of Caeiro is entirely hidden by that of Campos. This is why

Sá-Carneiro is able to concede to Pessoa that its absence is justified, while at the same time completely regretting it.

The name of "Caeiro" is present as an imprint upon that of Sá-Carneiro. But, in the unconscious alchemy that presides over the naming of the master, another Portuguese poet, Cesario Verde, plays an eminent role. The third poem from *The Keeper of Sheep* is dedicated to him (we also find several allusions to him in the work of Campos). This poet, at the same time a man of commerce and a man of the countryside, despised by the intellectuals, remaining unknown his whole life, will die from tuberculosis (like the father of Pessoa) at 31 years of age.

Under this name, partially taken from Pessoa's friend, Caeiro possesses a personality and a life in which we find a blend of biographical traits coming just as much from Cesario Verde as Pessoa himself:

> Alberto Caeiro was born in 1889 and died in 1915; he was born in Lisbon, but he lived almost his entire life in the countryside. He had neither an occupation nor education. [...] Caeiro was of a medium build and, however truthfully fragile, (he died of tuberculosis) he didn't appear as fragile as he was. [...] Caeiro is pale blond, blue eyes. [...] Caeiro, I have said, had almost no education – only primary school; very early his father and his mother died, and he stayed at home, living off odd jobs. He lived with an elderly aunt, his great aunt (Letter to Casais Monteiro from January 13, 1935).

**Fernando Pessoa – himself**, the orthonym, is the author of an oeuvre designated by Pessoa as a *Cancioneiro* – which is to say, a volume of "chants", following the model of the *Canzioniere* of Petrarch. (Another less universally known origin of this form comes from the Portuguese tradition of the *cantigas* – a tradition attached to the movement of the troubadour-poets and by which King Denis, the poet king of the XIVth century, distinguished himself.) The exact form of this *Cancioneiro* never saw the light of day. Nonetheless, the poems supposedly belonging to it clearly distinguish themselves from the other poems penned by Pessoa, such as the *Quatrains in popular taste*, *Message*, or even the initial poems.

Only the poems written with the *Cancioneiro* in mind are designated by Pessoa as coming from the orthonym, and they are the only poems to be included in the *Fictions of the Interlude* – the title under which Pessoa envisioned publishing the four heteronymous oeuvres. Orthonymous poetry can be intrinsically recognized by its motor, which runs via the processes of doubling. The poetic orthonymous oeuvre is as sinuous as the oeuvre of Caeiro is transparent. The thought at times gets lost within its own labyrinth.

It is a matter of great consequence that one of the heteronyms is an orthonym. Eduardo Prado Coelho remarked that the existence of the poetic orthonym amongst the four does not signify the so-called "Pessoa" occupied a central position within the heteronymy: "We would be incorrect in imagining a Pessoa-himself at the center of the heteronyms," he highlights, "because this circle does not contain a center." The bearer of the proper name of the author is, from another point of view, affected by all types of singularities: no date of birth or death, no physical portrait (except indirectly due to its presence in the *Family Discussion*), no fictitious biography; the only traits mentioned are the ones ironically described and commented on by Reis and Campos.

**Ricardo Reis** is the author of a very considerable number of odes inspired by the Greek and Latin models, even within their syntactic construction. "He is a Latinist by the education provided to him and a semi-Hellenist by what he taught himself" and, in this way, he is identical with his creator.

Pessoa makes Reis born in 1887, thus two years before Caeiro – which corresponds to the real time displacement between the first sketch of Reis in 1912 and his birth as a disciple of Caeiro in 1914. He is supposed to have been born in Porto, become a doctor, and to have lived in Brazil beginning in 1919, having "voluntarily expatriated himself because he was a monarchist". Physically, "Reis is a bit smaller and more corpulent (than Caeiro), but dry".

He is an extremely delicate, rigorous, and severe analyst of the ensemble of the heteronymous poetic oeuvre and presents himself as beholder of a poetic aesthetic which has ethics as a driving force.

**Álvaro de Campos** is the author of an oeuvre that appears to be made out of two opposing parts (three if we count, as introduction, the artificial existence of a "decadent" poet, who, before his meeting with Caeiro, wrote poems in the style of "Opium Eater"): the grand initial odes are immense poems full of breath and ambition; at the other extremity, the "millimetric poems" struggle to keep discouragement at a distance which seems to be born out of the impossibility of repeating the fervor of the first poems.

Younger than Pessoa by 5 years,

> Álvaro de Campos was born in Tavira, October 15, 1890 (at 1:30 in the afternoon, as told to me by Ferreira Gomes, and it is the truth, because the horoscope was done for that exact hour). As you know, he is a naval engineer (from Glasgow), but is presently on leave, in Lisbon. Álvaro de Campos is big (1 meter 75 – 2 cm more than me), thin and has the tendency to slouch. All of them (Caeiro, Reis, Campos) are clean-shaven [...] Campos, whose skin color is some shade between white and brown, is a vague type of Portuguese Jew, but with straight combed hair, a part on the side, and a monocle. [...] Álvaro de Campos was an average student in high school; he was then sent to Scotland to study to be a mechanical and then a naval engineer. During vacation, he traveled to the Orient and it is from this trip he gets the idea for the poem, "Opium Eater". An uncle from Beira, who was a priest, taught him Latin (Letter to Casais Monteiro from January 13, 1935).

**The Family Discussion.** This project deals with an ensemble of texts in which the heteronyms argue for their respective poetry, judging, normalizing, and thus defining their own position within the quartet. A good number of these texts (which have the form of notes or which are made up from the re-transcriptions of fictitious discussions between the poets) are consecrated to the evaluation of the philosophical singularity of Caeiro's oeuvre.

The same desire gave birth to several sketches for a book of philosophy by a fictitious author, Antonio Mora. This book was to have a title Heidegger would have enjoyed, *The Return of the Gods*. But the *Family Discussion* remained merely at the level of sketches, and the book by Antonio Mora never saw the light of day.

The non-convertibility of heteronymous poetry into a philosophy verifies itself in its non-deployment of the "philosopher-heteronym" – he remains in the shadows, without proper oeuvre -, but also within the impossibility of transposing the poems of *The Keeper of Sheep* into a philosophical discourse internal to *The Family Discussion*. The impasse becomes transparent in the subtle mixture of wonderment and deception instilled in the work of his fictional interlocutors, via the philosophical prose of their master. It is impossible to substitute a philosophy for the thought the heteronymy configures from the interior of poetry. The lone path of approach is in carefully reading, contemplating, and examining the poems.

All the texts from *Family Discussion* try to attract attention to the importance of what is at stake in heteronymous poetry. They are positioned around the oeuvres like buoys alerting one of a difficulty, obstacle, or turbulent waters. But they are powerless in exclaiming any better than Caeiro, Reis, Campos, or Pessoa what their poetry thinks, and to do so would be to fall into philosophical categories which are foreign and prior to them.

Through these fictive polemics, through the different portraits, the personality of each poet and his invented life adds itself to his poetic production. The heteronymy doubles the poetic oeuvre of these figures of fiction. It short-circuits and blows up any vision of the oeuvre as coming from any so-called "ego". It is from then on established that the "I" who is writing is another.

# 4

# Project of a metaphysics without metaphysics

Caeiro, above all else, proceeds in identifying metaphysics from the point of view of the poem and its interior operations. He does not proceed in this identification as a philosopher. His anti-metaphysical utterances have an efficiency which is intra-poetic. They are not philosophical equations conveyed via the poem. He tries to determine the principle of distance necessary from poetry vis-à-vis metaphysics: contrary to Campos who distinguishes philosophers by their names, because he is their interior interlocutor of an always silently followed conversation, Caeiro, uses the word metaphysics in a generic way, without ever setting his sights on a philosophy or specific metaphysics. He is, above all, critical and ironic vis-à-vis the poets who lean up against metaphysics like those unaware that the board against which they lean is rotten and has for a longtime been gnawed through. For his part, he tasks himself with producing a poem separated from metaphysics even its material.

The first separation Caeiro attempts to establish is this: there exist two regimes of thought. A "metaphysical" regime of thought which one should get rid of at all costs, because it consists in seeing behind a thing something other than itself, or merely apprehending a thing according to its signification, its meaning, and not according to its existence. And a non-metaphysical regime of thought which is the proper exercise of the poem in that it forces itself to "see without thinking", to see the thing to the extent that it is this thing and not another. This gaze is the asceticism offered up to the poem. Caeiro is the immaterial Keeper, the keeper of thoughts that make up his flock, because they are thoughts which distinguish themselves from the "thinking" of metaphysics.

It is in light of the poetic result that the critique of metaphysics should be appreciated. Caeiro's work is not about creating a philosophical system that would substitute itself for the rejected metaphysics. What is at stake is the poem the way the Keeper "writes it on paper which is found in [his] thought". That being said, we can unpack via the reading of the ensemble of the volume, and more specifically poems 2, 5, 9, 24, 35, and 39, quite crucial in their material, what Caeiro means by "metaphysics". The ambivalence of his own position as poet – responsible for loosening up the poetic tongue of metaphysics, but also with poetically fixing a non-metaphysical ontological path – discretely resonates from the first lines of *The Keeper of Sheep*: "I have never watched over a flock / But it is as if I had" – an enigma which will only be clarified in the 9th poem: "I am a keeper of sheep / The sheep are my thoughts".

For Caeiro, any relationship to the world and the universe that shows itself in terms of knowledge on one hand, and as a search for truth and meaning on the other hand, is metaphysical. As poem 5 states, the Keeper judges ridiculous and erroneous any "idea" of things, but also any thought in terms of "cause and effect", any contemplation on "God and the soul and the creation of the world", or still the "mystery of things", of their "intimate constitution", or their "inner meaning".

Strictly speaking, this is the type of method which forms what Caeiro calls "thinking", and he will contrast it with a freed "knowing how to see" that in some ways would be cleansed of a metaphysics that conceals the world of interpretations and prevents access to its pure contingent exteriority.

To break with metaphysics is to both accept the absolute exteriority of the universe and the world, and to recognize that their existence is not laid out for us, nothing is destined, and nothing can be contemplated from the point of view of some sort of meaning. Caeiro gives a name to this exteriority and non-interpretability essential to the world and the universe. The name: "things". We can argue that "things" is the poetic name of being, like the poem of the Keeper that strives to think without "thinking", that is, other than metaphysically. Once again, the exercise is poetic and in no way philosophical. Its unique tension is found within the relationship between "things" and the "visible". "Things" are what is seen by the poem as things. They are indissolubly what exists and what exists within the gaze of the poet who is capable of seeing in them, their naked existence. Here one should not understand "things" as a pure empirical given, but as the name of a poetic operation which is also ontological. Moreover, each utterance of the Keeper is not concerned with some sort of particular thing whose singularity the poem would try to grasp, but with the poetic conditions of what it is to see in a thing, the thing alone and not something else. The poems of the Keeper strive to stipulate what it is to "see", what distinguishes a "thing", rather than showing things in the ordinary sense of the word.

If we examine poems 10, 28, 35, 36, and 47, which explicitly critique the metaphysical leanings of other poets, we obtain a very clear view of what Caeiro intends to bring forth from his intra-poetic rupture. First, one must break away from an entire regime of poetry within which, according to the Keeper, perhaps the totality of poetry finds itself engaged and which consists of making one thing the carrier of another. Poetry of metaphor of course does this:

> Ah let us not compare anything at all, let us
>     gaze
> Let us leave behind, analyses, metaphor,
>     similarities
> To compare a thing to another is to forget
>     this thing.
> No thing recalls another if we give all our
>     attention to it.
> Each thing only recalls what it is
> It is only that which nothing other is.
> It separates itself from others the fact that it
>     is it.
> (Everything is this nothing without anything
>     which it is not.)

says one of the *Detached Poems*.[3]

The same can be said with symbolic and mystical poetry. This is the sense of the winged dialogue of poem 10 about the wind: a lie in making the wind say anything other than what it is, "wind only speaks about wind". The same thing can be found in poem 28. It is madness to attribute feelings to stones, rivers, or flowers. "Stones are only stones, / [...] rivers are nothing other than rivers, / [...] flowers are only flowers" (*"as pedras são so pedras / [...] os rios não são senão rios, / [...] as flores são apenas flores"*: three nuances of negative delineation follow one after the other, while the absence of the indefinite article in Portuguese allows for a latitude in translation as "stones are only stones" or "stones are nothing but stones" – my own choice punctuates the conviction that for the Keeper, it is not about tracing back the object "stones" to the essence "stones"). Poem 47 stigmatizes a category that we can find quite strange, that of "false poets". What is a false poet? It is a poet who designates the world under the name of "Nature" in order to bring to it some sort of meaning, even if this meaning is of an as yet still undeciphered "Great Secret" or "Grand Mystery". That Nature does not exist, that it is a metaphysical imposture to which a great number of poets have become accomplices, is after that of "things", the second discovery of the Keeper.

We will fulfill this vision of rupture Caeiro strives to create in referring to poems 14, 29, and 46 which attempt to describe Caeiro's process of the poem – without omitting

---

[3] *Oeuvres poétiques*, éd. by Patrick Quillier, preface by Robert Bréchon, Paris, Gallimard, from the collection "Bibliothèque de la Pléiade", 2001 : 84.

the recognition by the Keeper of his partial failure in keeping the register of the poem where he wants to establish it (the poems 26, 27, and 31 where he answers in advance the objections of non-accordance with his own ideal). The poem must simply conform itself with the being of things. The imperatives of writing are not artistic – that is why Caeiro can openly make fun of the poets "who are artists...", but ontological. Everything in the poem must present itself in an identical scheme to that of things. Thus, if the Keeper "does not worry about rhymes" it is because it is very rare to have "two equal trees, one next to the other". There is no reason for the poem to bear this mark of regularity. The ideal is for it to be able to "flourish", that what is written is as "natural as the emergence of wind". Here it is not about hailing the return of an inspiring Nature, it is a return to the things of the Keeper, all the things of the countryside that are small in number: flowers, stones, rivers, paths, hills, grasses, trees, rain, sun, clouds... The "inequality" of Caeiro's production is itself an image of a universe without unity, grasped always in the surprise of an emergence:

I am not always equal to myself in what I write and say

(*The Keeper of Sheep*, poem 29)

In this manner or another
According to whether it arrives or does not
Sometimes having the power of saying what
    I think,

And other times saying it poorly or with
    mixtures
I go on writing my lines unwillingly
As if writing were not a thing made of

gestures
As if writing were a thing that happened to
  me
Like taking on a bit of sun which strikes
  outside.

(*The Keeper of Sheep*, poem 46)

Without regularity of rhyme or rhythm, the poem tends towards prose: "I write the prose of my verse", Caeiro says, "and I am content". Paradoxically: language, words, and above all, the names themselves, are problematic for this poet. Not only does naming things fix them within something beyond themselves, it prolongs them above and beyond their existence. Not only do names mislead: as with the word "dawn" being betrayed as "an abstract thing, as a state, and not as a thing", the Keeper proposes to replace this "fake name" by "We are beginning to see the sun". But more profoundly still, words are in part linked with "thinking" and with that which in thought exceeds "seeing". Caeiro also dreams of the possibility of "directly referring words to the idea", and of no longer needing a "hallway of thought for words" ("*encostar as palavras à ideia / E não precisar dum corridor / Do pensamento para as palavras*"). We are surprised here of not finding "words directly referring to the thing". But here we are not dealing with the idea in the Platonic sense, but simply the idea in its most ordinary meaning of "that which occupies thought". One of the detached poems arrives at the conclusion: "I am not even a poet, I see."

## I

## The Keeper of Sheep
## and some Detached Poems

## Things

Being is not at all withdrawn, not at all out of reach, the whole of Being is visible, and nothing other than the visible exists. Such indeed is the blinding conviction of Caeiro, his founding illumination. All his poems affirm that from Being nothing is hidden from us, because it is itself nothing other than the visible. The word "Being" – inherited from metaphysics and, by consequence, banished from the lexicon of Caeiro – moreover is not sufficient: Being for him should not be the object of a general appointment. Rather than saying, when speaking about Caeiro, that Being is "things", it is better to say: for this poet, only things are.

More decisive still is the inclusion within the visible of the thought that thinks it: the distinction between Being (*l'être*) and being (*l'étant*) can be done away with once the schism between being and the thinking of being can be terminated. The visible for Caeiro should not be understood as that "which is seen", but as a non-subtractability of being from thought founded on the homogeneous character of thought and being.

### Soap bubbles

This is what his poems utter in varied ways, each one remarkable in its insightfulness. Things "simply exist". They "are what they are". They "are really what they seem to be". Things are without mystery: "What we see from things are things." This last affirmation refuses to dismiss them to the status of appearance, of an appearing or semblance. "Things" – transparent, says poem 25, or diaphanous, like soap bubbles – exactly equivalent to what we see in them:

> They are what they are,
> With a plump and aerial precision,
> And no one, not even the child who
>     abandons them,
> Claims that they are more than they appear
>     to be.

Furthermore, examine another poem, "why would we see one thing if another thing was there?" In substituting itself in the work of Caeiro for the canonical question "why is there being rather than nothing?", this question provides metaphysics with a sabbatical. The ontological displacement made here is considerable. Being is not a thing distinct from things – which would refer back to the interior of metaphysical categories, to treating Being (*l'être*) as a being (*l'étant*) amongst others; but it is not a thing among things either: it does not indicate a sign in the direction of a supreme or primary being, nor towards a withdrawn or veiled being. It is "things". Things are being in immanence with itself.

## The butterfly

What for Caeiro is indeed "a" thing? What distinguishes it, or identifies it, as "thing"?

The first thing that singularizes a thing is its radical absence of attributes: each thing exists within the interior of its own limit and distinction. The paradoxical and provocative utterance of the poem 40, "Butterflies have neither color nor movement", is crucial in this respect. The poem develops its argumentation in the following way: "The butterfly is merely a butterfly", while "it is color which is color in the wings of the butterfly" and, "in the movement of the butterfly, it is the movement which moves itself." The idea of the limit is thus essential: each thing is finite; it finishes there where another thing begins, discernable in its turn as such.

Under these conditions, would the butterfly, flowers, stones, the tree, or the river represent in the poetry of Caeiro the level of the metonymies of "things"? No, since each thing is what it would be, metonymy itself being a thing. Metonymy is an impossible figure in this poetic work.

Second decisive utterance – belonging to poem 9 from the *Detached Poems* – is the following: "To be a thing is to not be susceptible to interpretation." Why is this utterance essential? Because it fixes the regime in which things exist within the interior of the thought that thinks them. Indeed interpretation is identified here as that by which metaphysical thought, in "adding" a meaning to things, relates to their existence as a heterogeneous exteriority, opening at the same moment the hypothesis that they would possess some hidden secret. If things are not what they seem to be, things in themselves would differ in what they are for thought, or in the thought that thinks them. This path is energetically refuted by poem 39 from *The Keeper of Sheep*: "Things do not have a meaning, they have an existence", it is declared. From which, as a consequence, "things are the unique concealed meaning of things". To claim with such sharpness that it belongs to being as "things" not opening itself up to any interpretation whatsoever, supporting no meaning, and making no indication towards a signification, has as its corollary that nothing distinguishes the being of things from their being for thought. It is not that things are, as is the case in phenomenology, disposed "for" thought. It is precisely the opposite; their exteriority to the thought that thinks them is absolute. But it is nonetheless affirmed that thought can think them for what they are. There is no need to identify them beginning with anything other than themselves – that this "other thing" is a signification, referred to language, or to meaning, emanating from a hidden or supreme being.

If "things are real and each completely different from one another", the mode of existence of things itself demands to be understood "with eyes, never with thought", as poem 16 of *Detached Poems* repeats. Because to "understand this with thought would be to find all of them identical." In other words, to understand via thought, what is found within things would cancel out their proper being, their singularity. This is why any general naming of Being in the thought of the Keeper is inappropriate, but it is also here we find the core problems which the poetic ontology poses and against which he strives to develop a thinking counter to metaphysical ontology.

The poet follows a narrow path. If things are what Caeiro says they are, what is in fact the thought which would think them? To utter the heterogeneity of their being and of the being of thought is not enough. We must still identify the possible effective processes of such a thought.

## The figure of the "Keeper of Sheep"

All the pastoral figures have circulated in bucolic poetry with the status of abstract figures: artifice, allegories, and masks. The sheep themselves are purely symbolic, most often representing the thought of the poet. Caeiro inscribes himself in this tradition: do not some of his poems evoke, not without mockery, "the shepherds of Virgil" (poem 12)? But Caeiro is also a bucolic poet *of a complicated species*. His nickname, gently out of context, attests to this. *Keeper of Sheep*, this expression which gives its title to the major corpus of the poet, strangely resonates in Portuguese just as much as in French. The word used does not refer to the shepherd or to the pastor. The Keeper is not an allegory taken from tradition; he incarnates and bears the "thought without metaphysics" of which he and poetry prove themselves capable.

As the first poem of the collection describes, the Keeper sees indifferently when he "looks at his ideas"; his gaze finds his sheep, and when he looks at his sheep, his ideas take the place of his animals. In gently inflecting the classic metaphor – in which the accent is put on the reversibility between idea and sheep – Caeiro displaces the attention in the direction of a bizarre equivalence: that of the idea and the gaze. As is often the case in his work, the staging of symmetry creates a subtle disequilibrium, by which new thought passes. To gaze at ideas as we gaze at sheep? That this is possible from then on places the gaze under the sign of thought. But at the same time, thought itself finds itself designated as visible.

## There is thinking and thinking: thought and the act of thinking

However, thought and gaze first violently oppose each other in the work of Caeiro. For him, thinking is the contrary of seeing. He affirms, not without disgust, that thinking bothers him, thinking is the equivalent of being "sick in the eyes" (poem 2). Because "thinking" is, in the eyes of this poet, that which prevents all access to being. "Thinking" transports "an entire metaphysics", which opposes itself to whatever within the gaze sees the world and the being as such. The Keeper maintains the world pre-exists language; it is shielded from any signification; it expresses nothing: it is. This naked existence neither supports nor lays out any meaning whatsoever; it only attests to itself. And yet, "thinking" hands the world over to a transcendental investigation whose ultimate pursuit is God, creation, or the soul. "Thinking", under these conditions, is the equivalent of "not understanding", showing itself as incapable of grasping the world as pure existence. The Keeper critiques both a "thinking about" (*penser à*) made up of heterogeneous entities – such as the world and consciousness, the inner and the outer, the subject and the object, or still cause and effect – and a "thinking of" (*penser de*) this self consciousness of thinking where its initial heterogeneity is exacerbated. The task of the poem is to substitute for this thought lost in transcendence and the heterogeneous a poetic gaze trained to see and capable of grasping being. If the pensive herd over which this strange Keeper watches gather "contented thoughts" (poem 1), it is because they can take their contentment from being thoughts withdrawn from thought.

In fact, while the sheep of the Keeper are in appearance nothing more than his ideas, these ideas or thoughts receive, starting with the first poem in the volume, a singular acceptation: they are what the gaze produces, what the gaze of the poet "sees". In this regard, if the ideas of the Keeper can be placed amongst "sensations" (poem 9), we must still underline that in the work of Caeiro sight is the one sense which identifies thought. And the gaze, even more than sight, has an enormous privilege within this poetry. It is, of course, much more than an organ of sensation. It is that which at the same time opposes "thinking" and opens itself up to the non-metaphysical exercise of thought. It is also in this gaze, "clean as a sunflower", that the Keeper recognizes himself.

### The "savoir voir"

Caeiro thinks "with his eyes and ears /And with the hands and feet / And with the nose and mouth" (poem 9), but the essential, he insists, is to "know how to see". This illustrates quite well that the seeing of the poem is neither clairvoyance nor vision, nor the simple spontaneous seeing. Seeing is the contrary of thinking, in as much as the gaze proves itself capable of being a thinking different than the sad thinking of metaphysics. Its exercise demands the poem to rid itself of all previous apprenticeships; it successfully achieves this by a persistent, focused, voluntary effort of the abandonment of all learned forms of thought. The poem of Caeiro strives to materialize the constant and vigilant exercising of such a gaze, which frees thought from metaphysical influences and gives access to being with a new vigor and innocence (poem 2).

In this framework, the injunction "to not think when we see" is quite easily comprehensible. But it is followed by a more obscure interdiction: "nor see when we think". Here thought progresses anew by the introduction of a subtle destabilizing symmetry. The two successive utterances attempt to define the conditions of possibility for exercising a non-metaphysical thought. The demand to "know how to see when we see" underlines the fact that the gaze is the lone site possible for a non-metaphysical or anti-metaphysical thought. Thus it is about not letting oneself reintroduce "thinking" within "seeing". The gaze should be entirely and purely the gaze. There is no thought without metaphysics as long as thought is not integrally this "knowing how to see" (*savoir voir*) within which the poem of Caeiro exerts itself. To embark in "seeing when we think" would be to fall back onto learned "thought". Because whoever would claim to see, at the same time as he thinks, would most certainly see nothing at all, nothing of what a thought in rupture with metaphysical vision strives to capture. Thinking and a gaze without metaphysics are unique unto themselves. Indeed the gaze of the Keeper proposes a thinking which is not "thinking".

## Moonlight

The poem is the instance when things are thought, or can be thought, as the things they are. In this sense, the poem is the lone site of the visible. But it can only become as such in getting rid of all that previously made up the poem and any trace of its metaphysical relation to the world.

Such a major change engages multiple precisions and delineations concerning what the poem should be, in opposition to the poetry of those Caeiro describes as the "fake poets", and those he attacks as "mystical poets" or "artist" poets.

According to the Keeper, there exists an essential collusion between poetry and metaphysics which he sees himself capable of ending the moment from within in his own poems that stones, flowers, rivers, and trees are merely viewed for what they are: things which simply exist. Caeiro sticks by this figure of innovation and rupture at the interior of poetry, because all of his predecessors inscribe poetry in the figures of meaning. Which he summarizes from an extremely precise equation under his apparent ingenuity:

> The moonlight through the high branches
> The poets say is more
> Than the moonlight through the high branches

> (*The Keeper of Sheep*, poem 35)

It is this "more" which takes as its target the poem of the Keeper, which strives to stick with the thing itself. Against the expressive and interpretative slope of the poem, Caeiro does not back down in front of the burden nor sarcasm:

> The poets say flowers are sensations,
> And they say stones have a soul
> And rivers have raptures in the moonlight.

> (*The Keeper of Sheep*, poem 28)

The Keeper identifies within the expressive character of poetic operations a figure of thought connected to metaphysics. If he rejects poetic expressivity, it is because he attributes to things a meaning which is intrinsic to them. In the secret controversies with poems from admirable predecessors – Leopardi, whom Pessoa knew and admired[4]; the English romantics, Wordsworth, Shelley, Keats; or even the Portuguese metaphysical poets, Antero de Quental, Teixeira de Pascoaes – the poetry of Caeiro labors to eliminate any poetic figure which would bring into being a meaning, whatever it may be. These confrontations remain underground. In particular, they are never nominal, because the ambition of the Keeper is not as much to designate adversaries as it is to clearly distinguish between two regimes of the poetic. He attempts a rupture: it is about taking one more step, a step outside the poetic.

As long as metaphysics organizes poetic art – and the poem 10 of *The Keeper of Sheep* shows with elegance how this takes place – the poem is incapable of being the tight exercise of seeing that Caeiro advocates. Expressivity introduces an "ulterior motive" within the figures, and things become the support of meanings which are foreign to them. According to Caeiro, poets lie when they bring a meaning to things in their attempt to fill the world via meaning. Poetry, according to him, is declared to be wholly responsible for a falsification of Being. Thus the poem sees itself subdued by a double tension: on one hand, it is identified as the archetypal site of metaphysical distortion;

---

[4] Pessoa dedicated a poem to Leopardi which he began in 1934: "Canto a Leopardi", in *Obras de Fernando Pessoa*. Porto, Lello e Irmão Editores, 1986, t. I, *Poesia*, p. 406, and *in* Fernando Pessoa, *Obras poética*, Rio de Janeiro, Nova Aguilar, 1983, p. 450 and 451.

on the other hand, it is required to be the eminent site of the visible. It becomes impossible without a poetic rectification or reconstruction. Does the oeuvre of Caeiro complete this rupture whose necessity it proclaims with such great force?

There is no doubt that his oeuvre shields the world and thought from all transcendence and signification of meaning. But is there really an untangling of Being and the One within these poems? Do they escape the transcendence that could be called immanent, a transcendence that continues to keep Being under the grasp of a One even if this One would no longer be a causality or an intrinsic meaning, but a simple trait of Being? To put it another way: in what way does the "thing", according to Caeiro, exceed the reciprocity that seals together Being and the One? In what way is his poetry not a pure and simple reiteration of the utterance of Leibnitz "what is not One being, is not a BEING?" It could be that the poem of Caeiro says the stone exists only to the extent that it realizes, in language, the "one" existence of this stone. Established in a polemic, the poem of Caeiro is very often the injunction and declaration rather than effectuation. Is it able to go beyond the incitation to "see" in order to truly work on a transmission of the "visible"?

If this poetry does not effectuate this untangling of the thing and the One, it should be recognized that it has failed, that it remains hostage to a metaphysical mode of thinking which it struggled to succeed.

## The flight of the bird

There exists, for the poem of the Keeper, for the gaze which is his, no other possible mode of grasping things than in a vision of them "always for the first time". Because, "to remember" is already to no longer "see". To remember is to penetrate anew within the register of consciousness and to part ways with the imperative of the gaze. That each thing must "be whatever it is" – as poem 12 from the *Detached poems* notes – but also nothing other than what it is, thus imposes that things be extracted from all temporality. If only the thing alone exists, void of the "beyond" or "below", this beyond and below which would constitute its perpetuation, its existence in duration, would not know how to be a part of it as well. Thus we must assert that each "seen" thing is a new thing, and give to this utterance all of its radicality.

What is seen is in no way the same thing seen anew:

> What I see at each moment
> Is what I have never seen before
> And I know to be very attentive to this.

The "each time" of the seen thing is thus not deduced from Time: all that exists is an eternity of things, their always new existence within the gaze which captures them. Eternity here is the unexpected corollary of the radicality of emergence and the impossibility of repetition. Poem 43 utters: "What has been is nothing." In the ontology of the Keeper, the past is devoid of being, not being a thing. Still more radically, Time does not exist. This emerging eternity of things within sight gives them an extraordinary intensity, which is not their empirical glare, but the ontological vertigo of a thought capable of seeing a "thing" within what it sees.

Being "very attentive to this" is to again understand that the thing for Caeiro does not echo any substantial identity. Not only is it not an object for a subject, nor an appearance referring to an essence, but its existence as thing only is only one with the "what is seen", while – this second point is essential – it is nevertheless a pure exteriority for the gaze which captures it. Here, it is not privy to its intention "for it". It is thus a double "movement" of the gaze, which is capable of seeing without thinking (or if not, does not see), and of the thing (seen each time anew) to which the "thing" devotes itself.

The multiplicity of things is no longer the empirical multiplicity of the world from which abstract unities would detach themselves. It is the incommensurable multiplicity of the "each time seen". The thing in its inseparable being of its "being seen" only has an existence as an unlimited multiplicity. The "always for the first time" of the thing and the gaze multiplies to infinity the "things" well beyond the finite capacity of seeing them. And from this infinity, as poem 41 rejoices, "There must be many a thing / For we have much to see and hear…"

This bi-junction of the thing and of the "what is seen" evades the allocation of the thing to the One. It follows that the poetic gaze must be, according to the wishes of poem 43 from *The Keeper of Sheep*, "rather the flight of the bird which passes and does not leave a trace / than the passage of an animal which leaves a memory on the ground." If the thing is the "what is seen", thought cannot be the memory of what was seen, since on the one hand, that which is, is always a "what is seen for the first time" and, on the other hand, what is no longer seen no longer is. It is this being of the thing with which the gaze-thought of the Keeper complies. The difficulty which arises is that this thought, as such, is not "naturally" spontaneous. Not only because it has to escape from metaphysical thought, but also because the character of thought as a thing is not capable of being entirely "like" things. Metaphysics aggravates this incapacity, which, on the contrary, the anti-metaphysical poem, strives to reduce and absorb.

### The lone poet of Nature

In poem 46 from *The Keeper of Sheep*, Caeiro blissfully credits himself with a discovery: the elucidation of the "Great Secret" or "Great Mystery" to which the "fake poets speak". The explanation consists in the following: there exists no possible recollection of things in one unique entity, an entity whose name in poetry has always been "Nature". Poem 47 utters this with a perfect clarity in an impressive succession of theses:

> I *see* that there is no Nature,
> That Nature doesn't exist,
> That there are mountains, valleys, plains,
> That there are trees, flowers, grass,
> That there are rivers and stones,
> But there is not a whole to which all this belongs
> That real and true unity
> Is a sickness of our ideas.
> Nature is parts without a whole.

The multiple being of things is here declared a rebel against all totalization: the "things" of Caeiro exist in an absolute dissemination within this "there is" which the poem is able to match by accepting to see it each time anew. The extent of Caeiro's conviction that metaphysics incarnates a diseased thought is perceptible in these lines. The vocation of the Keeper is to heal thought, to release it from its sadness and metaphysical turmoil. In this manner, Caeiro is related to Wittgenstein, as therapist of philosophy.

It is not without irony – this ingenuous irony of the Keeper, which gives him the voice whose intonations are almost carnal – that Caeiro proclaims himself "the Discoverer of Nature" (poem 46), or better still, "the lone poet of Nature" (poem 16 from *Detached poems*). As in the case of the word "thinking", he introduces here a polysemy of the word "Nature" with which he plays. He no longer comprehends it in the way it was used in poetry influenced by metaphysics, but in the anti-metaphysical sense of the word which is his own. This polysemy thus authorizes the paradoxical utterance according to which the lone poetry loyal to Nature is that which is inspired by the conviction that Nature does not exist.

"Nature", as the Keeper thinks it, is "without-One". What he is content including under the name of Nature, from then on, merely gathers up parts which between them compose no group or totality whatsoever. This is a new bias by which the "things" of Caeiro escape the influence of the One. Indeed, it is very important that they not only constitute a multiple figure, but that in this fragmented multiplicity, no unity can be composed. What the category of Nature supports here is the character of non-totalization of the multiple. That things are not identifiable as substance or beingness (*étantité*) leads the Keeper to definitively utter that there exists no natural figure of Being. Anti-metaphysical, the poem of Caeiro establishes itself within an a-cosmic figure of Being.

## Names and things

In looking at this absolute dissemination of things, what role then does naming and language play? Would it not be through them that the One returns? Because on the one hand, names generalize and, on the other, names necessarily perpetuate things above and beyond themselves. Caeiro confronts this difficulty head on: he announces that fundamentally, "things have neither name nor personality, they exist" (poem 27). Thus, ideally, the poem should also shed itself of all already existing names which, in order to name things, are nothing but "signs" placed onto them. For example, such is the case, according to poem 45, for the words "row and the plural of trees", because "they are not things, they are names". Do names exist capable of not exceeding the things they designate? This is the question.

"In truth," Caeiro maintains, "people should give a different and proper name to each stone. As we do for men; we do not do it due to the impossibility of having enough words, not because it would be an error to do so." This solution, whose limit is manifest in that it would paradoxically compose a non-language, without forgetting to acknowledge what Jean-Luc Nancy calls in his work the "idioms" of things.[5] By the tension that it introduces, it

---

[5] See Jean-Luc Nancy's works such as *A Finite Thinking*, Stanford University Press, 2003. *Being Singular Plural*, trans. Robert Richardson, Anne O'Byrne, Stanford

highlights that the problem is the result of "Nature", as Caeiro identifies it, not being a language. "It is not at all a language", poem 31 underlines with vigor. "Things" resist the naming of language because they are, in the vision that Caeiro gives to them, radically inexpressive: they "correspond", contrary to what another poet (Baudelaire) maintains, to nothing, not even a name. Every name, in order not to be in excess of the thing, in order to always be exact, must be subjected to this "always for the first time" which is the common law of the existence of the thing viewed and of the gaze which grasps it. Thus the problem is not found on the side of things but on the side of language, which does not know how to conform itself to the being of things.

The singular poet that he is doubts language at the same time affirming that the poem is the closest in capacity to naming each thing in its exteriority and uniqueness. The poem alone knows how "to be very attentive to this", or rather – because the poem is also capable, according to Caeiro, of being exactly the opposite, which is to say, of being the site of the metaphysical expressivity and ulterior motives – it can force itself to be very attentive to this. In this trilogy where "the thing" is absolutely primary and language is almost superfluous, what is a poem? It is of course, first and foremost, the site where, as poem 13 reminds us, we do not know what we are thinking nor do we strive to know. A negative operation of subtraction from the grasp of metaphysics. But if we scrutinize the positive allocations of the poem, we find very little: it must be the

University Press, 2001, or *The Sense of the World*, trans. Jeffrey S. Librett, University of Minnesota Press, 2008.

site of simplicity, a calm, "natural" preciseness which would be the result of its capacity to "only see what is visible" – utters poem 26. These very strange lines from poem 41, however, shine light on the kind of impasse or aporia where Caeiro retreats with respect to language:

> Ah, the senses, the sick who see and hear!
> Could we be as we should be,
> And there would no longer be any need of illusion...
> It would be enough for us to feel with clarity, with
>     life,
> Without even worrying about the senses...

"To feel with clarity, with life", such will be the ideal operation of the poem, and this is an operation which does without the use of the senses. It will discover here that "seeing the visible" has little to do with perceptible vision. To see the thing as thing is not to see an "appearing", but the thing in its being, which is its lone existence. For the Keeper, the being of things does not have an "appearing". The word "things" is destined to dissolve this distinction; it designates the undividable overlapping of being and appearing. The powers of language would matter to the poet if he wanted to capture being in its appearing, because language would be the mediator in such an operation. But Caeiro asks nothing like this from the poem; he implores it to indefatigably show that there is only being and that this being is accessible to thought once thought organizes itself around and submits itself to the inexhaustible multiplicity of things. The poem is thus the site of trying to be "as we should be", the site of conforming men and things.

## Mysticism or poetic ontology

At the same time that poetry is denounced by the Keeper as a major supplement to metaphysics, philosophy is disqualified for him in that

> With philosophy, there are no trees: there are only ideas.
>
> (*Detached poems*, poem 1, "It is not enough to open the window")

To be more precise, we never encounter within philosophy "what we see when the window opens". To put it another way: Philosophy is radically deprived of access to things in the way that the poem is capable of grasping them and making them be seen. The principle accusation, which Caeiro makes against philosophy, is that things and ideas do not co-belong to the field of the visible. The figure Caeiro targets under the name of philosophy, and which is more specifically *Platonism*, is terribly autistic. In Plato's philosophy:

> There is only each one of us, like a cavern.
> There is only a closed window, with the world
>     outside,
> And the dream of what could be seen if the window
>     opened,
> And which is never what we see when the window is
>     open.
>
> (*Detached poems*, poem 1, "It is not enough to open the window")

Thus philosophy introduces a disaccord within the visible: what we see when the window is open is not what we dream we could see if the window were open. It is quite remarkable that the critique of the Keeper does not reveal, in the philosophical operation, an opposition between the perceptible and the intelligible, but a discontinuity in the interior of the visible which is indicated by the double status of the window: from the interior of philosophy the impossibility of the window opening in such a manner that we could see it is postulated, while the movement of the poem is synonymous on the other hand with the window opening. If all the thoughts of philosophies on being are inappropriate, it is because they are incapable of recording anything other than the gap which repeats between the dream they propose of the visible and what springs forth as irreducibly singular in the seeing. For the Keeper, philosophy is presented foremost as dreaming, incapable of exposing itself to the radicality of "each time seen".

## The interpreter of Nature

As it is for the philosopher, it is more so for the poet of things who is also not entirely exempt from inaccuracy. Indeed, he finds himself forced to being "this odious thing, an interpreter of Nature."[6] What leads him to this is the heterogeneity of things and language highlighted earlier. The poet is necessary precisely "because there are men who do not understand its language [which is that of Nature], because it is not at all a language" (poem 31). If the philosopher is an autistic figure, the figure of the poet is presented in his manner as a schizoid figure: in order to merely make men "see" what things are, the poet is obliged to use language. He must translate for them what he "sees"

---

[6] There has been a persistent error in the deciphering of this line. The first Portuguese editors transcribed it as: "I am this *serious* thing, an interpreter of Nature". This error still appears in the Gallimard edition of *The Keeper of Sheep*. *Le gardeur de troupeaux*, trans. Patrick Quillier, Editions Gallimard, 2009.

in things at the same time being certain that this translation distorts and deforms his thought.

The being of things not being integrally transmissible by common language leads to the poetic necessity of translating it. Their recalcitrant beings have something ineffable: the poet, who so strongly challenges interpretative poetry, becomes their obligatory interpreter.

### The risk of a mysticism

Caeiro does not back down from the accusation of mysticism. It is not a mysticism which would reintroduce the figure of the divine or transcendence. This mysticism is easily broken up by the ontology of the Keeper: "I do not believe in God, because I have never seen him", says poem 5, and he continues:

> This may seem ridiculous to the ears
> Of someone who does not know what it is to look at
>     things,
> Does not understand who speaks about them
> In the way which observing them one learns how to
>     speak about them.

It will appear clear that any divine figure can be reduced and defined from the point of the visible. To suppose that a god exists, he would himself indeed be necessarily a thing and subjected to the rule of "seeing". The last words of Caeiro are not that God is dead, but that he is sleeping. This is, at the least, the last line of the last poem in *The Keeper of Sheep*: "And there, outside, a great silence like a god sleeping."

We should not, on the other hand, let the heterogeneity of man and Nature, man and things, be reduced to that which the hiatus of language bears witness. The new difficulty is the following: if thought itself is a thing, it nonetheless possesses, as a thing, a distinguishable singularity. This singularity is that it is not able to achieve this perfect exteriority to itself which is peculiar to things.

Does this characteristic really identify thought as a thing, or is it an illusion of thought, the shadow of the incapacity of thought to consider itself as a thing? The Keeper seems to sometimes hesitate on this point. On one hand, he maintains things do not have an interior and, in this regard, ourselves "prior to being interior we are exterior". This is explained very soundly in poem 32 of the *Detached Poems*. He concludes: "And from the beginning, we are essentially exterior." But, while Nature does not have an inside", thought presents itself as the thing whose singularity is found in the fact that it cannot be devoid of all interiority. Nature is said to be "divine" according to Caeiro, due to its capacity of being purely a thing, which is to say, pure absolute exteriority. In this regard, it is non-human or more than human; it represents ideally what poetic thought should be. The possibility of a poetic mysticism exists because there must be a voluntary effort by the poet in order to overcome the hiatus which manifests itself between the perfect natural exteriority of things and their interiority (whatever its origin finally is), which affects his thought to the extent that it is a thought.

Caeiro declares with his typical precision:

> My soul is simple and does not think.
> My mysticism is not wanting to know.

(*The Keeper of Sheep*, poem 30)

In pondering these lines, we will notice that the poetic figure is primary and immanent: "My soul is simple and does not think". This is the privilege of the poet. Starting with this announcement, we can begin to construct a kind of "reverse cogito" of Caeiro: "I am there, where I am not thinking." The mysticism is second: it proceeds from the self-consciousness of thought, from what it uncovers in thinking itself, by the singular capacity of thinking itself. The poet realizes that what animates him is a "not wanting to know" – another way to put it, a voluntary effort to equate his interiority with the pure exteriority of things – and at the same time he discovers the partial incapacity of his thought being equal to things.

It is impossible for the poet to completely avoid mysticism, but he has the freedom to discern it within himself and limit it. The poetry of the Keeper applies here. It has an ability of appeasement to the extent that it fully renders justice to the exteriority of things and the universe, including man, as poem 32 from the *Detached Poems* magnificently proclaims:

> Peace to all pre-human things, was this within man,
> Peace to the entirely exterior essence of the
>     Universe [...],

The famous poem 8, because it sets the stage for the links between the poem and the divine, sketches out a demarcation between this always possible mysticism and the poetic ontology which the Keeper attempts to found.

### The intervention of poem 8

This poem reflects upon the poetic process itself. Its central affirmation is that poetic capacity presupposes mediation.

The one who is presented as providing the poet access to "all that exists" is a child described with the traits of a child-like renegade Jesus, a graciously puerile village divinity. This child who is both eternal and new, this Christ estranged from Christianity, fiercely skeptical about the existence of a creator God, having fled the boredom of the sky, having abandoned the hollowed imprint of his body on the cross – this Christ, from then on, partakes in the sacrilege and mischief of the rustic life of the poet. In regarding this figure, we think of the child of *Zarathustra*, but more probably still to the enigmatic intervention of the goddess towards Parmenides:

> And the goddess, looking into the future, received me favorably, from her hand
>
> She took my right hand and told me the words,   singing for me...

The whole poem brings to light the mediating character of the child who, following the goddess of Parmenides, "takes a hand" of the poet and with the other hand "all that exists". He is the one who taught the Keeper to "look at things": is it not the direction to which his finger points that indicates at each instant where the poet should pose his gaze?

Pessoa, on several occasions has insisted on what amounts to, in his eyes, the troubling character of this poem, including the reason that it was written while in trance state. In reading it, its charm resides in a fantasy, a spectacle, an abandon, which evoke texts written as "automatic writing".

There exists in the ontological project of the Keeper a development of the impossible. This development resides in the desire "to be entirely my exterior". This capacity, which even the poet does not have at is his disposal, is described as "divine" – in the same manner Nature is described in poem 27:

> Only Nature is divine, and it is not divine...

The capacity to hold thought in the exteriority of things is thus designated as divine; next, this name is crossed out so it does not summon up some sort of transcendence or figure of signification. This same operation of citation-erasure, which we could also name "repenting" (in the manner it is used in painting: a trace which deliberately remains visible after a touch-up of the initial design), is repeated concerning the child-god who is the gauge of the poetic labor of the Keeper:

> We live joined together
> By an intimate agreement
> Like the right hand with the left

This figure first emerges in a reference to Christ, but this reference is then point by point undone and deconstructed. The divine name thus becomes the name of the only active and living pure fiction when its neglected icon is relinquished "to the sky" like an empty metamorphosis.

Incarnating "the human who is natural" – this improbable chimera – the divine child gives to the Keeper the ability to see the world as he sees it. In the end, this child, Caeiro declares, is nothing other than "my daily life as a poet". It is also "because he always walks next to me that I am still a poet". The figure of the child indeed presents the poetic process itself to the extent that it shows itself capable of providing a non-metaphysical "vision" of things.

Caeiro makes this mediating fiction of the child surface as the indication of an irreducible differentiation between thought and the thing it thinks. From then on, the poetic ontology of the Keeper presents itself as a tension directed towards an evading "simplicity", and as a desire to conform thought itself to the existence without mystery, interiority, and meaning proper to "things".

## The apprenticeship of unlearning

Such an ontology necessarily follows a hazardous path. It is, in effect, the tributary of the poem of which it is the unique instance and whose success is each time aleatory and necessarily unequal: "I am not always equal to myself in what I say and write", warns poem 29. The poem 46 explains this in its own way:

> In this manner or the other
> According to which it is good or bad
> Sometimes capable of saying what I think
> And other times saying it poorly, all mixed up,
> I go on writing my lines without wanting to.

The Keeper obeys this "non-wanting" which is essential to the poem: neither the "non-wanting" of any poem, nor that of "inspiration" – but the exigency of not being within the element of a wanting to think. This non-wanting relies on a double ascetic. Thought first has to rid itself of everything it has learned and peel itself away from all false sensations, which prevent it from seeing things and Nature in their calm exteriority. Then, according to the Keeper, the thought of the poem must carve its path by directly applying "words to the idea" without passing by a "hallway of thought for words".

These images from poem 46 create, from the first encounter, several difficulties. What can "applying words directly on the idea" in fact mean? And what is this "hallway of thought" one should avoid? Does this exigency target a preformed vision within thought it would impose on words? It seems the difficulty can be removed if we admit that the proposition examines the poems of the Keeper in their materiality. The poem is made up entirely of words, unlike Nature which, as we have seen, is not language. The poem is thus necessarily in a position to translate, but it transposes into language something which is not a language.

## The Hallway of Thought

Are we dealing, via the poem, with an extension of Caeiro's principle of a tendentially idiomatic naming of things? It would seem that he does not engage himself on this path. What is essential for Caeiro is that the poem resists the reduplication of the idea by the conscious. Thus, it has to escape the reflexive interiorization of the thought it carries. This is how we can understand the necessity of avoiding the "hallway of thought" in which the idea is threatened to be lost.

To break with all reflexivity is to hold the poem, its writing itself, under the law of the exteriority of self, which is that of things, and this seems to be the goal of the Keeper. Indeed his poems do not claim to inscribe the existence of things, nor their pure presence as things. The poems of the Keeper rather liberate each time the site and the equation of what it is to "think things as things". They thus transmit an exercise of the gaze, the conditions for a thought which is not thinking, or still its asceticism. They are the poetic indication of what it is to shield thing-thought from metaphysical thought. As in the work of Parmenides, rather than the poem clarifying entirely an orientation for thought, it indicates a direction while at the same time forbidding another.

## The voices of the poem

The clearness, the precision, the limpidity, the translucence of most of the poems of Caeiro come from operations whose principle production comes from a linguistic tongue, which goes outside the intimacy of the written, constantly making the voice of the poet heard as a voice which talks to itself in front of everyone, or which speaks out loud, with all the immediacy and suppleness and possibility of recovery or hesitation at the disposal of a voice.

It is first and foremost from the plausibility of this strange "written voice" that the strength of the fiction of the Keeper emanates. It is a solitary persona, walking just as well in the sun as in the rain, accompanying his flock, always thinking, muttering, speaking like shepherds who live alone have custom to do. Having hardly been sketched out this figure is quickly denounced and shown as fictive: "I have never watched over sheep" – such are the words offered up for reading immediately after the title of the volume. "*Keeper of sheep*" is itself a name-thing, an absolute singularity. And the apparently non-fixed, uncertain character of the voice, of the different voices each poem lets speak, deepens the weight of each thing said.

On the other hand, it is from this character that we discover the extreme difficulty of reading his poems out loud: because what timbre does the voice of Caeiro have? And what are the voices to which he objects or responds? It is impossible to read his work without entertaining some answers to these questions.

### The "prose of my verse"

The poem presented in voice has all the precariousness of speech. It affronts a certain risk of misaddress, it allows itself to correct itself. If the voice corrects itself, it is during the course itself of what it utters or because it is returning to its first utterances. This projection of voices in thought is comparable to the emergence of each poem, of the "always the first time" emergence of things within the gaze. The poem professes thought rather than writing it. It leans on the exteriority of speech in order to keep thought, by the power of the vocal, from the error of any interiority with itself. If we had to give a figure to this name, it would have to be possible to speak about "exterior monologues".

This manner of construction sends the poem to the border of the poetic and the non-poetic, to the limits of prose. Caeiro is perfectly conscious of this when he says:

> To be a poet is not an ambition that I have

> (*The Keeper of Sheep*, poem 1)

I am barely a poet: I see

(*Detached poems*, poem 12)

I write the prose of my verse
And I am content

(*The Keeper of Sheep*, poem 28)

This inclination of the poem towards prose is by no means, in his eyes, a flaw or weakness. It is commanded by the thought of the poem, which, breaking away from metaphysics, must also break away from a certain regime of poetry and more fundamentally from the concept of poetry as art. The quarrel of the Keeper with the other poets is definitively based around the existence of such an art in their work:

And there are poets who are artists,

poem 36 states ironically. Caeiro accuses this art of the poets of introducing in the poem the ulterior motives of metaphysical thought – whether in the sense of a beyond inherent to the symbol or the double meaning of metaphor.

Poem 39, developing the idea that things are truly what they appear to be, highlights that this ontological proposition, in respect to things, is "stranger than all strangeness, and all the dreams of all the poets, and the thoughts of all the philosophers." It is precisely in striving to let the strangeness of this new thought be seen that the poetry of Caeiro forces itself to create a new regime, without art, of the poetic. To work his lines like a woodworker works his boards, to place them line by line, like bricklayer constructs a wall, "and see whether it is good and to take it off if it is not"; this is what Caeiro cannot do.

He opposes the artistic poets with a flourishing of the poem: "What a pity it is to not know how to flourish!" But what is "to flourish"? On the one hand, no doubt it is to keep the poem in the constantly improvised element of the exterior monologue and of its voices; on the other hand, it is to not be decided *a priori* as for the delimitation of the poem and the prose, allowing for the thought of the poem to perform its own separation within the prose.

### The separation of the poem from art

It is this novelty to which this expression refers, "I write the prose of my verse", that requires another look. It contains the idea of a deliberate limitation of the poetic by the poet: the desire of a "proximity" between thought and things does not exactly demand a "prosaism" of the verse, but an imprint of prose on verse. What is this internal "prose" of the poem if not the manifestation that thought is not a subjective instance. We understand, if it is about showing a non-subjective identity of thought and the thing it thinks, one has to separate the poem from art. Because, art, by the requisite forms it takes, is the instance par excellence of subjectivity. But to separate the poem from art, one is obliged to shield it from any formal injunction, and in accordance with this precise point, it is rendered homogeneous to prose whose existence, contrary to poetry, is informal.

It has often been insisted the use of tautology would create this effect of prose and would thus make up the specific language of the Keeper. To which would be added a transverse organization to the poems of argumentation – which gives to *The Keeper of Sheep* the character of a short and dense "treatise" and not a simple volume of poems. And yet, rhetorical categories such as "tautology" prove to be inadequate and hollow. When Caeiro indeed announces "a stone is a stone", it is clear he does not limit himself to saying the same thing twice. The second term of the proposition does not reiterate the first. The enunciation creates a differentiation: a stone is a stone, which is to say, nothing other than itself. Essence and existence are given as joined and not separate from one another. Here, the figure of thought is a letting happen, in the gaze, of the exact identity of the thing with itself.

The absence of rules concerning rhyme is another "prosaic" trait which Caeiro proclaims. There are, properly speaking, no rhymes nor non-rhymes in his work. His poem thus manages to conserve itself as poem in passing outside the requirements of punctuation, whether internal to the line or in a forged distance with the existence of the line. The poem of the Keeper is formless. This point is of extreme importance. Poem 14 explains its significance:

> I think and write like flowers have color.

Two lines should not be any more similar than two trees. If there is not a systematic omission of rhymes nor, as a consequence, free verse in the work of Caeiro, it is because it is not about following a poetic process, but putting to work a decision of recklessness. This decision being the only one likely capable of rendering the poem exact in its proper being, which is to say, homogeneous to the thing. It is about trying to conform, as much as possible, the being of the poem with the being of things. What guides the poem in the work of Caeiro is not at all an aesthetic canon, but an ontological principle.

Conversely, it is the power of the ontological principle which keeps the poem of the Keeper on the side of the poem, which prevents its transfer purely and simply into prose. In its nakedness, the poem of the Keeper thus exhibits the element that separates poetry and prose: prose pivots around truths, the poem, around Being.

## The heteronymous master as separatory power of poetry and philosophy

"What does not have limits does not exist. Existence implies something else and by consequence that everything is limited. [...] Is it so hard to conceive that a thing is a thing and not another thing which prolongs it indefinitely?" Caeiro argues in a debate from *Family Discussion* (*Notas para a recordação do meu mestre Caeiro*) which distinguishes him from Campos. The thought of things here hinges on the idea of existence and that of the limit; any figure of infinity is, on the other hand, absent. Would the thought of things in the work of Caeiro then be a thought about finitude? Should we comprehend it, in borrowing an expression from Jean-Luc Nancy, as a "finite thought"?[7]

### "I am the dimension of what I see"

It is the implicit decision of the Keeper to do without infinity – a choice that Campos and Reis will consider a

---

[7] *A Finite Thinking*, Jean-Luc Nancy , Ed. Steven Sparks, Stanford University Press, 2003.

Greek trait, an archaism, and can also be considered as a mark of modernity. The infinite cannot be engendered starting from a finite figure from the world and thought. To establish the infinite thus presupposes to propose another vision than those devised by metaphysics.

In the work of the Keeper, that each thing is finite is not a clause of finitude. The assumption of finitude generally proceeds not from the existence in the self of the finite, but from an interpretation of the finite as incomplete and from the will to reabsorb this incompleteness or from the desire to give it meaning. And yet, the Keeper announces, on the contrary without ambiguity, that "to be complete, it is enough simply to exist" (poem 12 from *Detached poems*). That each thing exists according to its own limit nowhere means that "things" are "finite". In this ontology, there exists no immanent principle of finitude, because there exists no possible recollection of things in a unique ensemble: there are merely "some" things, which is to say, a multiplicity in itself without limits. Here, we measure the extreme importance of Nature being defined as "parts without a whole".

This principle of completeness, if it opposes itself to the idea of finitude, does not in all this open itself up to an infinite figure. "I am the dimensions of what I see / And not from the dimension of my own size" (poem 7): "I am the dimensions of what I see" indicates that if the poetry of the Keeper is not a "finite thought", it does not however contain the infinite. Because the same way the finite does not in itself contain finitude, so it is with the inconsistency of things: the multiplicity of the multiple possesses in itself no principle of infinity. It is with a complete awareness that the poet presents himself as the "Discoverer of Nature". It is with a touch of anti-romantic irony that he proclaims himself, in poem 16 of *Detached poems*, "the lone poet of Nature". He can add to this: the most contented poet in the world.

> I bring to the Universe, a new Universe
> Because I bring to the Universe itself.

In reality, the pair finite/infinite is dismissed by Caeiro like all the other metaphysical pairs (idea/sensation, exterior/interior, subject/object, etc.). The poem of the Keeper places itself edge to edge with the Universe – a Universe whose exteriority is total, no longer susceptible to being interpreted, and which articulates no meaning – a thought of the Universe no longer a parasitical victim of meaning. In this regard, this poetry indeed pronounces the end of any cosmogonic or pantheistic figure of the infinite. That it does not propose any other figure becomes of great consequence concerning the question of the infinite, which from then on seems to come from a singular and intrinsic ontological decision. The poem susceptible to materializing a new thought of the infinite would not be identical to the poem which strives to think things as things. The poem of things and the visible stops and another poet appears: no longer Caeiro, but Campos.

## There is quite enough metaphysics

Let's address to the Keeper the questions that Heidegger posed to Nietzsche's Zarathustra, since, like him, he is both an "essential figure of the thinker" and the theme of a poetic creation:

> Who is this master who is teaching? Who is this figure who
> appears in metaphysics at the stage of its completion?

If the Keeper's quarrel is with metaphysics, it is because the question of Being, above all others, is at stake: can the poem carry a thought of Being which is not a deceptive metaphysics incapable of grasping Being in its real existence? While there is an air of controversy in and around the poems, Caeiro only risks posing this question because he is certain of receiving an answer and is assured that it represents a rupture and an innovation. Poem 5 from *The Keeper of Sheep* deploys the meditation.

"There is quite enough metaphysics"...it is with these words that the decisive poem begins:

> Há metafísica bastante en não pensar em nada.

> There is enough metaphysics in thinking about nothing.

> (From the French Translation
> of Rémy Hourcade, Éd. Unes)

- There is quite a lot of metaphysics in non-thought.

> (From the French Translation by
> Armand Guibert, Gallimard/Poésie)

The two translations of this line distinguish within the work of Caeiro an imperative of "thinking about nothing" (that Guibert dared even to name "non-thought"). We are not dealing here with a non-specific thinking about nothing. It is quite right that these translations put the accent of this line on what was designated as the will in the work of Caeiro of a thought that would not be thinking, a thought that would be a "non-thinking". The subject of this inaugural line is to highlight that even this non-thinking contains within it metaphysics.

Moreover, the rest of the poem does not allow it to be understood any other way, since it opposes this metaphysical branding of the most shielded thought from metaphysics to the perfect absence of the metaphysics that belongs only to things to the extent that their existence is entirely un-conscious and un-known to them.

- There is enough metaphysics thinking about nothing.

(Trans. José Gil[8])

- It is enough metaphysics to think about nothing.

(Trans. *Pagan Poems*,
Christian Bourgois)

- There is quite a lot of metaphysics in thinking about nothing.

(Trans. Teresa Rita Lopes[9])

These three translations do not, however, clearly identify the "thinking about nothing" as a singular maxim of the Keeper and do not indicate in what sense this poem is a quarrel Caeiro has with himself with the hope of producing a thought distanced from metaphysics. The translation of Teresa Rita Lopes, moreover, weakens this affirmation: this line is not a simple offhand comment of disillusionment, but a vigorous misplaced declaration.

---

[8] In *Fernando Pessoa ou la métaphysique des sensations*, Paris, Éd. de La Différence, 1988.
[9] In *Fernando Pessoa, le théâtre de l'être*, Paris, Éd. de La Différence, 1985.

To think about nothing, in itself, contains everything one needs from metaphysics.

(Trans. Dominique Touati, Éd. de La Différence)

This last version is the product, however, of a double counter-meaning: Caeiro appears to congratulate himself – perhaps ironically – that there is metaphysics within thought and, at the same time, finds himself proposing an exercise of thinking about nothing which would however be the metaphysical exercise par excellence. This interpretation cannot be maintained.

The entire poem constitutes a sort of manifesto at the heart of the volume of *The Keeper of Sheep* against onto-theology, which is designated as the obvious or secret core of all metaphysical thought. And, from the manifesto, this text has a tone and vivacity: the poem does battle with diverse interlocutors, standing up to all objections. What matters here is less to take up one more time the analysis of what Caeiro means by "metaphysics" than understanding how, in his eyes, the relations between the poem and metaphysics articulate themselves.

At first glance, the metaphysics which the poems of the Keeper critique and deride could be seen as entirely foreign to his own work. The metaphysics which he identifies and pokes fun at is that of the other poets: it belongs to a poetry which links being and existence to an extreme mystery, attributing meaning to things, connecting the existence of the world to causes and endings. And the poets who are its principle peddlers are so due to their love of double meaning, metaphor, and symbol – all figures that carry within them the inscription of metaphysical dualism.

The first movement of this great poet is to pit against these poets the non-validity of the totality of their questioning. For the Keeper, "to think about these things is to close one's eyes and to not think". A thought of Being similarly subjected to the categories of metaphysics is not worthy of the name thought. It must be put aside for the benefit of the lone thought this poet considers as thought: that which passes by the exercise of the gaze and whose place is his own poem.

Only sickness can lead it back to metaphysical wanderings:

> What do I think about the world?
> If I became ill, I would think about it.

Caeiro, moreover, did not miss the chance of writing four poems by the sick poet in order to show how this state affected his thought. (Poems 15 to 19)

### Ontology, metaphysics, and poetry

Nonetheless, it appears to be difficult to entirely separate the poetic ontology found within the poem of the Keeper from the metaphysics it opposes.

Poem 5 maintains there exists no "better metaphysics" than that of the trees, because it consists of "not knowing why they live / And nor do they know they do not know." These trees do not appear as metaphysical symbols, but rather as the incarnation of the metaphysical ideal, something like the best possible metaphysics, a metaphysics of non-thought. Contrary to these trees, the Keeper is compromised by a mysticism to the extent that his thought would only ever be but an approximation of this radical non-thought. In order to think of nothing, to become a thought that exempts itself from thinking, the poet must voluntarily produce an attempt.

There is perhaps not so much a pure and simple rejection of metaphysics in the work of Caeiro but the desire of bringing to light and from a distance, a particular metaphysical configuration: that of a circular dualism between philosophy and poetry which prevents the poem from latching thought and things onto the regime of the "visible". If the poetry of the Keeper does indeed operate on a rupture with metaphysical dualisms as it does with onto-theology, does this breach as such not remain definitively internal to metaphysics?

This is what the second movement of this same poem 5 attests, consecrated to proofs of the existence of God. The Keeper does not engage in a direct refutation of transcendence but a patient reduction of the question with the help of the ontological category of "things", according to a demonstration in three sequences. First sequence: I do not believe in God, because I have never seen him; and yet, only that which the gaze captures is a thing, and only things have an existence. Second sequence: but if God is flowers, trees, mountains, sun, moonlight, as a certain poetry maintains, then I believe in him. Third sequence: Nevertheless, if this is the case, should we call him "God"? If he is nothing other than things, there is no need to think of him as another thing than them. Poem 6 will again refine this idea of God as a thing among things in affirming that

God is this thing which does not want us to know it. The poetic ontology of the Keeper accords no other identity to God than that of thing. Because of this, the name "God" finds itself crossed out rather than denied: divine superfluity is affirmed rather than its inexistence or falsity. The poem of the Keeper is thus able to separate poetic-ontology from onto-theology in showing that no Supreme Being is necessary; thinking about things is enough.

Metaphysics and philosophy do not appear to entirely overlap neither within the critique nor the poetic apparatus of Caeiro: if the separation between ontology and philosophy is clear, the constitution, however, via the poem of a new ontological figure, is the product of a site which is not radically separated from metaphysics. This leaves in suspense the question of exact relations between the poem and anti-metaphysics, or non-metaphysics, on the one hand, and the distinction between philosophy and metaphysics, on the other.

### The project of a metaphysics without metaphysics

The work of the Keeper separates poetry from philosophy in affirming the properly poetic singularity of the "gaze-thought" of the Keeper. *The Keeper of Sheep* is not a new philosophy, and Caeiro does not propose to poetically restructure philosophy. He declares, rather, that ontology must be shielded from philosophy and assigned to the poem. It is about installing a poetic location of the thinking of Being that is not only "anti-metaphysical" but above all "non-metaphysical". And it is from the interior of poetry that this rupture must come.

The critique of the collusion between poetry and metaphysics must be via poems. The "gaze-thought" of Caeiro is a thought of things that is able to reject dualism and thus succeeds metaphysics. In this regard, one should give him a place amongst the other revolutions of all orders which were created at the same moment, such as cubism, Leninism, or relativity. This new capacity of the poem constitutes the position of mastery that the Keeper holds at the heart of the heteronymy. The works of his disciples Reis and Campos are homogeneous with this vision; the orthonym alone pits against Caeiro's things the existence of what he calls "no – things".

The poetic oeuvre of the Keeper announces less the end of metaphysics than the end of a certain configuration of metaphysical thought. The Keeper forms the project of what it is possible to call a "metaphysics without metaphysics", to the extent that he "keeps" from metaphysics all that can be kept, which is to say, its ontological ambition. Would it not be him, this "Esteves without metaphysics" who exchanges a saving smile with Campos at the end of the *"Tobacco Shop"*?

The *sou contento* of Caeiro – an "I am content" which evokes the meaning of joy in Spinoza – is the final color of thought whose grace makes it that

> Something relaxes in us
> And accepts everything more clearly.

(*The Keeper of Sheep*, poem 25)

## II
### *On the six love poems of Alberto Caeiro*

No more so than *The Keeper of Sheep*, the *Shepherd in Love* does not present himself as a conventional bucolic figure. He constitutes rather the figure of a litmus test via the love of the ontology of the Keeper. We sense that in the eyes of Caeiro, what is the most singular in man is his thought, to the extent that it is thought which distinguishes him as a thing amongst things. Is love a thought? And what is this thought? Or is love a dispossession of thought under the effects of something which is foreign to it? An aggravation of the non-exteriority of itself from thought? The landmarks given to the fictitious life of Caeiro are 1889 and 1915. *The Keeper of Sheep* is dated by Pessoa 1911-1912, even though the first poems of the volume were written in 1914. The same time-shift exists for *Detached poems*, dated 1913-1915, while the conception of most of the poems took place between 1915 and 1920, and then during the course of 1930.

From the six poems, unpublished while Pessoa was alive, which make up the volume *Shepherd in Love*,[10] only the first two are dated 1914, but are we dealing here with a fictitious or real date? The four others, all from 1930, compose a small veritable cycle: indeed three of them share the date July 10, 1930, the fourth, July 23, 1930. These poems, regarding the "life" of Caeiro, are essentially "posthumous" poems. They are essentially his poems from beyond the grave. All things considered, the figure

---

[10] The reference is made here to the corpus presented by the Édition Gallimard/Poésie. The Édition de la Bibliothèque de la Pléiade proposes a different corpus.

presented by the title is not exactly that of the Keeper: a tiny heteronymy in the interior of the heteronymy, in love, the Keeper becomes the "shepherd". It is not irrelevant that the cycle of July 1930 of the *Shepherd in Love* is entirely after the revival of the love of Pessoa for Ofélia Queiroz. The latter recounts in *Letters to a Fiancée* : "We began our *"namoro"* again. It was in 1929 [...]. We wrote and saw each other until January 1930." The debut of their love covered the whole year of 1920, but Ofélia adds: "Even during the nine years in which we practically never saw each other, I believe he never stopped loving me." From 1930, there are several notes with different dates by Campos on the subject of a certain woman, who remained unknown to everyone, whom Caeiro loved: "Let her remain anonymous, including to herself", says one of the texts uncovered and published by Teresa Rita Lopes in *Pessoa por conhecer* (t. II, p. 478).

These dates must be close to those of the genesis of the *Quatrains*. Henri Deluy, their translator, remarks that after the first eight poems which probably go back to 1907-1908, "twenty-six years pass, if we believe the dates of the exhumed papers, before Fernando Pessoa begins to compose the rest of the quatrains". From July 1934 to June 1935, on the other hand, he writes several hundred of them. And yet, Deluy writes, "most of the quatrains are love poems".

All presence of love in Pessoa's life has been denied. We have attributed a "blank sexuality" to him, which is to say, a fundamental incapacity to love transcending in him all sexuality. And yet, the majority of the *Quatrains*, added to the volume, *Shepherd in Love*, constitute, in regards to love, some profound and singular thoughts.

Love does not present itself in these poems as a transport outside of self, but a type of intensification of self. Love intensifies thought. It does not trouble thought, nor steer it away from what it thinks; it gives it new colors and vibrations. In the work of the Keeper, whose singularity as a poet is "seeing", it is above all the gaze which is intensified by the proximity of love:

> I see rivers better when I go with you
> Through the fields to the banks of the rivers;

And:

> Seated next to you observing the clouds
> I observe them better.

Love, thus, does not distance Caeiro from his thoughts on things and the world: "You have not taken Nature away from me", he says. Love, on the contrary, allows him to get closer to what he has to think: "You have brought Nature, close to me, very close." Why? Because of the fact of love, Nature sees itself positioned "very close to thought", instead of within the external distance to itself. Love operates a reduction of the gap between Nature and the thought that thinks it. Thus, it is not that under the effect of love the being of Nature changes; it's the gaze-thought which becomes more acute:

> From the fact of your existence, I see it better but identical.
> From the fact of your love I love it in the same way but more.

The love of the *Shepherd in Love* is more generally the instance of the Same: neither the beloved nor the world become other from the fact of love; nor more so than the existence of love is the internalization of different thought. To be chosen by love, to be the site of love, simply yields a new capacity: it performs an extension, an accentuation, an intensification of the attention of thinking, via its gaze of things:

> From the fact that you have chosen me to love you and have you,
> My eyes have fixed themselves (on Nature) in slowing themselves down in seeing all things.

The *first poem* of the *Shepherd in Love* marks with its extreme probity its own site: to examine the effects of the existence of love on the poet.

This love does not belong to the realm of being but of having:

> At the time when I did not have you
> You chose me to have you and to love you.

The "having" and "not having" creates two different times. This "having" results from the love to come. The "having" here exists neither as essence nor calculation. Love is given, encountered without anything dictating it. It is different from being. It is heterogeneous to it. One should thus say: love is not a "thing". This heterogeneity of love as having, however, does not modify anything of being. This is why the time anterior to love is not a time dictated by error or wandering, no more so than the time of love undermines the being which precedes it. On the contrary, this love authorizes the poet to persevere in his own being:

I do not repent for what I once was
Because I still am this.

In addition, since the choice is that of the other, it is incalculable. And yet, only this choice precedes the birth of love: "You chose me to love you." – not in order to make you love, nor to be loved – says the poem with precise words. Here, love is thus not a well tried sentiment, but the constraint of an exterior choice, to which it is only possible to consent or not consent.

It is very surprising to notice that nothing, in this first poem, identifies a man or a woman: the masculine and the feminine are nowhere to be seen, not even grammatically visible. The figure of love designates, in a low-key manner, lovers; it cuts-out silhouettes, suggests them without showing them. And, however, it is obvious from the first poem that there are two interior positions of love. On one side, there is initiative and choice; on the other, the acceptance of the encounter, its recognition as encounter. The poem maintains that love operates a sort of new signaling (*aiguillage*) of thought to the extent that it is a love of what thinking thinks. So it is that love would modify the register of thought, its "affectivity". In the past, the thought of the Keeper loved Nature "like Christ does a calm monk"; from the interior of love, the comparison becomes: "like a calm monk loves the Virgin Mary, religiously in my way", which is to say, "in a most moved and close manner". Thus, there exists a kind of non-sexual sexuation, induced by love, in how thought thinks.

The *second poem* opens with a declaration which challenges the loving lyrical romanticism:

I think of you, and I feel myself complete.

The poet adds almost as quickly this nuance:

I think of you [...] and I am not me [...].

In this love, he calls himself complete and "not me". This "not me" implies that he is no longer himself once he is happy. Happiness thus distinguishes itself from the *sou contento* of Caeiro. Happiness, nor more so than the love which creates it, is of the register of being and things. It is an accident or event.

In this poem, a dissymmetry directs the acts of love:

Tomorrow you will come, you will go with me to pick flowers from the countryside.

And I will go with you into the fields to watch you pick flowers.

There is "to pick flowers" and "to watch you pick flowers", and these obviously cannot be exchanged: each image is in the interior of the Two of love.

"It will be a joy and truth for me": a joy but also truth. Love, contrary to the thought of being, comes from truth. When it gave itself over to one of the two in thought, however, love was only a feeling: a feeling of completeness at the beginning of the poem; then a feeling of happiness in the thought of the next day.

We are dealing with the capacity of proving oneself complete no longer in the register of being but existence. The Keeper maintains, "To be complete, it is enough simply to exist". Nowhere is love represented by the

Shepherd as a privation of oneself, an exile outside of thought, an alienation of the self in the other. On the contrary, it is what manifests the complete character, self-sufficient from its own existence.

*The third poem* – here we are talking about poems from 1930 – is a pure gem. Love, not the lover or beloved, is company, the poem maintains. In love, even "absence is company". This company is definitively that of love and not some aleatory presence of a lover. We are "with" love. This indicates love merges not with being but with existence. It is an existence which adds itself to existence, this is the reason it can be there "forever". This quite beautiful word "company" again designates a presence which does not come from a desire: "I can no longer go anywhere alone." Love accompanies each one of us; it is not described as something split or even shared, but as a company that the existence of each lover singularly and irreversibly grants to the other.

> If I go alone, I see far less
> Due to a visible thought
> Which makes me go faster
> At the same time giving me a desire to see
>     everything.

All thought, to the extent it is itself a thing, belongs to the visible. What other poet is capable of rendering thought as present as a thing?

A new "visible thought" is what makes up the company of love. This thought is added to the visible without contradicting the positive effect of love, which in increasing the desire to "see everything" nonetheless troubles the view. Under the effect of this thought, the poet goes faster, thus he sees less. This visible thought which is love jostles the thought of the visible that is the singular thought of Caeiro.

There is amongst other things, the quandaries of love and desire, the clairvoyant realization that desire, far from being homogeneous with love, obstructs it, and that the body in a sense is always a "foreign" body.

Love must pass by desire, traverse it, even if desire is infinitely more narrow than love:

> I love her so much that I do not know how to desire her.

The emotion, the trembling, the proof of presence undoes the consciousness of "that which is composed of my experience in its absence." Desire is a force of the imagination:

> If I do not see her, I imagine her, and I am strong
> Like the tall trees.

When he finds himself in the presence of the beloved, this force "abandons" the poet. Tying desire and love together, this is also the first poem where the feminine is explicitly legible. The following comes to Caeiro from the interior of love: "All reality watches (him)." In the sunflower of the Keeper appears the face of his beloved woman and, by a sudden reversal, reality begins to watch the poet who watched it.

In the *fourth poem*, the allegorical figure of the Shepherd returns under the name used as the title of the ensemble of the six poems: *The Shepherd in Love*. This is a critical poem. Love threatens to destroy the poet: all his thoughts are scattered out onto the hills once "in trying to think" he stopped "playing the flute" in order to gather them up. In truth, the Shepherd, in trying to think about love, forgot the poem. He lost his guiding force, he lost the ability to still unite his thoughts: those other than the Shepherd gather up the sheep on the side of the slope.

What is this "thinking" that absorbs the Shepherd? What is it in love which steers him away from his own thought? Would the Shepherd have fallen back to a destructive "thinking" of those "thoughts" over which Caeiro watches – this thought of things of which one must be capable "without thinking about what I am experiencing"? What type of thought then is love?

In looking closely at this last poem, the thought which steers the Shepherd away from his thoughts is not love at all, but on the contrary, a skepticism in the place of love: nowhere else does the shepherd encounter the company of love; he doubts whether he ever had love: "Nothing appeared nor disappeared from in front of his eyes". Nothing took place. Are we dealing with something that happened or an illusion – "No one, in the end, loved him" – or even a bewilderment – "rising up from the slope and bewilderment". A bewilderment caused by a thought partaking in the thinking of the poem and the poet? It is due to this sudden doubt, this uncertainty, that love sees itself described here as "false truth". If the Shepherd turns towards "the entirety of reality", it is because it seems "more real than any feeling". He thus recovers, not without pain, a "freedom" – this "kind of freedom in one's chest" –

of which the feeling of love deprived him. The tension of the poem is extreme: it oscillates between relief that there never was any love, the negative freedom of returning to the real, and the pain of having to conclude that if love was nothing but a disruptive feeling, it was in a position of being neither thought nor truth.

The following poem, the *fifth*, operates on a reversal or even a raid (*coup de force*). This poem contains a crucial utterance: "to love is to think". It is an exit from skepticism. The crisis opened by the preceding poem finds itself affirmatively resolved. Love will not have been the false route of feeling. As difficult as it may be, one must struggle to name the thought that love is from the interior of the thought of things. On this condition alone love will find grace vis-a-vis the Keeper. Who other than he could say:

> I ask nothing of anyone, not even her, except
> thinking.

The poet will force himself to show in what manner love is a singular exercise of thought: on the one hand, he notices that it is composed of "thoughts with the memory of what (the beloved) is when she speaks (to him)". On the other hand, he highlights the fact that this thought which is love can be stronger than the thought of "feeling":

> I who almost forget to feel in front of her lone thought.

Love as thought is not identical to the thinking of things. "Seeing" for example, in love, becomes: "seeing her form outside of space", "and seeing it on different days than those when her real person appears to me." This obliges

Caeiro to admit, in this singular thought that is love, "thinking" and "gazing" can be separated. What is more, there is something in love which does not let thought rest, which activates it and endlessly nourishes it from its passion. Would this be desire? No, because love as thought designates that which comes from love and which precisely does not come from the indecisive opacity of desire.

As desire, love is obscure, but as thought, it is clear:

> I do not know well what I desire, even about her, and yet I only think about her.
>
> I do not know very well what I want; what is more, I do not want to know. I only want to think about her.

This "thinking towards" which is love, does it consist as a "thought about" love? In the same way that the thought of things is not a thought of an object, the thought of love is not that of an object, whatever it may be, not even of thought itself. There exists rather a thought *in* love. This reinforces the deep conviction of Caeiro that thought is neither reducible to knowledge nor science.

The *final poem* calls love. Despite the separation which has intervened between the lovers, we are not dealing with a poem of mourning, but one in praise of love. A poem to affirm it is good, that love is. The existence of love distributes love and pain, but also something more precious than the unique thought of things. This something which pushes the poet, separated from the beloved, to say:

> I have no use of my feelings.
> I have no use of myself, when I am my only company.

The Keeper, in truth, never had any use of himself, since the real is precisely what is not found in him. But love, which experiences "company", taught him that "self company" is nothing.

Love reconnects thought with awakening: "Before, I awoke with no feeling: I was awake." It is necessary in order to exist, "that someone tell me something", because it is only in this way, "I am awaken anew" to the world. Love always demands "to be awakened anew" to the world. Here resides its eternity.

Not that a love can't be interrupted. Not that separation and lost don't exist. But for those who have known love, it is no longer the feeling of self nor the unique thought of things or the world that matters, but the company of love to the extent that it is another very precious thought and, from then on, the companion for Caeiro of the thought of things.

Throughout the poems of the *Shepherd in Love*, the Keeper discovers that when truths are at stake and no longer Being, there can exist a thought other than the thought of things. This new delineation arising out of the distinction between metaphysical "thinking" and a thought which is not "thinking" is of enormous scope. Thought about Being and thoughts about truths stop coinciding on this point. The gaze-thought of the Keeper is a thinking about things, not about truths. That he returns to the poem to think "things" leaves open what can be considered truths and thought, or thoughts susceptible of thinking truths.

Such is the caesura that performs in the work of Caeiro, this brief but dazzling evidence presenting love as another figure of thought. The substitution of the silhouette of the Shepherd for the Keeper records this reorientation.

# 5

# The orthonymous challenge
# of the Two

We remember that the letter to Casais Monteiro presents the emergence of the poem "Oblique Rain" as the "reaction of Fernando Pessoa to his inexistence as Alberto Caeiro."

The orthonym "un-exists" from the moment Caeiro manifests himself. A sentiment of the creator, erased by his creation? Or are we dealing with the concealment of the poet Fernando Pessoa by the poet Alberto Caeiro? How should we understand that here where the thought without thinking of the Keeper establishes itself, the thinking of things, the poet by the name Fernando Pessoa immediately ceases to exist? What does the poem of the Keeper cancel, ignore, or deny in him? Does Fernando Pessoa belong to this metaphysical poetry for which Caeiro accounts? Conversely, does the maintenance of its poetic existence compromise, via the interior of the heteronymy, the master figure of the Keeper? It is impossible to respond to these questions without first clarifying two others: why an orthonym? What is the orthonymy?

## Why an orthonym?

A singularity of the orthonym which distinguishes it, as witnessed by the three other poets, is that it bears the proper name of their common creator. What meaning should we take from this trait? Does the orthonymy designate the non-heteronymy, the totality of that which is not written under the fictitious names of Caeiro, Reis, and Campos? If this were the case, we would have to conclude that "Fernando Pessoa" does not exist in the interior of heteronymous apparatus: the orthonymy would simply be the opposite of the heteronymy, or even its exterior.

But an all together different hypothesis is possible, one which consists in considering "Fernando Pessoa", to the extent it is an orthonymous name, as not being a real name subordinate to fictitious names, but as a fictitious name equal to the three others. The strangeness comes from the fact that this fourth name is not one more "other" name, but the inclusion of the proper name in the heteronymy as a fictional one. All decisions in the work of Pessoa being governed by a powerful ontological necessity, it is possible to conjecture that this orthonymy allows him to differentiate the heteronymy as creative power and not as a fountain of illusions: without an orthonym there would be no heteronymy, but merely a multiplicity of fake names. It will be the orthonymy which articulates the transformation of multiple names into a configuration of "other" names.

Beginning in January 1915, Pessoa confesses to Cortes Rodrigues his desire to make appear *"under a pseudonymous form"* what he will then name the "oeuvre of Caeiro-Reis-Campos". He writes to him about this (in a letter from January 19, 1915): "It is *a whole literature* that I have created and lived, which is sincere, because felt, and susceptible to having beneficial influences on other souls." In 1919, he questions himself again (writing this time to F.F. Lopez regarding a project of a revue in French and English) about the possibility of publishing under pseudonyms and, in this case, what the "aesthetic of the pseudonym" would be. To make the poems of a lone author appear under various pseudonyms would have amongst other benefits, in his eyes, to overcome the "numerically small amount" of Portuguese poetry which has counted over the last number of years. The lone category which presents itself is thus that of the "pseudonymy", and immediately the question of national identity finds itself linked to the multiplicity of other names, even though the heteronymy has yet to be identified under this name.

According to João Alves das Neves, in reality, we have to wait for the *Bibliographic Table* to be published in 1928 in the revue *Presença* for the name of heteronymy to be proposed as such. My own research does not invalidate this date. Thus, it would be 14 years after the apparition of the four poets that the distinction heteronymy/pseudonymy would have been formulated in complete clarity. Several points in this inaugural text from 1928 allude to this. First and foremost, the heteronym is assigned to Caeiro, Reis, and Campos alone:

> The heteronymous works of Fernando Pessoa are *made*, up until now, by *three people's names*: Alberto Caeiro, Ricardo Reis, Álvaro de Campos. These individualities should be considered distinct from their author. Each one constitutes a type of drama; each ensemble forming another one.

Thus the heteronym is strictly Trinitarian and subsumed under the name of the author. In the continuing text, certain links between the poets are established: Reis and Campos are described as disciples of Caeiro for the reason that each of them has "isolated in this work" a singular aspect of the orientation of the thought of their common master. On the other hand, the orthonymy, as the term appears, is defined without any more precision, unlike the "rest" of the work, be it prose or verse, to which Pessoa assigns some sort of value.

Definition in the tradition of Monsieur Jourdain:[11] Everything that is not heteronymy is orthonymy...

In 1929, some letters addressed to João Gaspar Simões distinguish between the poems "from me" and the poems from the "trans-me", those "existing now or in the future from Caeiro, Campos, Reis, and the others." He even adds an allusion to a "something from myself" which would be intended for volume number 27 of *Presença*! This proves that the heteronymy is not yet absolutely concentrated in the three poets at the same time the orthonymy is not truly identified as anything other than an autonomy ("me-me"). The name, in its strangeness, nonetheless exists as an opaque anticipation of what is at stake. The indecision of the exact delimitation of the heteronymy goes hand in hand with the impression regarding the contents or the nature of the orthonymy.

---

[11] Cf. *The Bourgeois Gentleman* by Moliere, "Everything that is not verse is prose and everything that is not prose is verse."

In 1931, the designation of heteronymy stabilizes itself. Pessoa crosses it with that of the "dramatic poet". The letter from December 11, 1931 to Gaspar Simões contains an exact description of the heteronymous processes:

> The central point of my personality, as an artist, is that I am a dramatic poet; Without end, in all that I write, I have the intimate exaltation of the poet and the depersonalization of the dramaturge. I vanish elsewhere – *voilà tout*. [...] As a poet, I feel; [...] as a dramatic poet, I feel in detaching me from myself; [...] as a dramaturge (without a poet), I automatically transmute what I feel into an expression which is foreign to what I felt, in constructing within the emotion a non-existing person who would truly feel it, and would thus feel, as a derivative, other emotions than me, which the one who is merely me, has forgotten how to feel.

On many occasions, Pessoa uses the metaphor of "the drama not consisting of acts, but of people" which would make up the heteronymy. This excerpt from the letter to Gaspar Simões has the honor of clearly indicating how the idea of drama and the heteronymous creation communicate: a "non-existent" person, forged in the exercise of the poem and comparable with, by its own existence, the theatrical persona, is the point of departure for an unheard-of poetic capacity. This fictitious persona, whose existence has the same power of conviction as a grand theatrical figure, is the dwelling of new singular emotions, which the creator, reduced to his own personality, has "forgotten" to feel.

We have to wait for the letter from 1935 to Casais Monteiro, the *Autobiography* of Pessoa (which is written during the year of 1935) as well as his ultimate plans of publication, in order for the orthonymy to be clearly assigned to the lone Pessoa of the *Cancioneiro* and for the orthonymous figure, thus isolated, to be explicitly included in the poetic heteronymy. The undated texts from the *Family Discussion*, in which the existence of the orthonym Fernando Pessoa is patently clear, would in this case belong to the same period. It is in these final texts of Pessoa, and in particular the letter to Casais Monteiro, that essential things find themselves clearly expressed: on the one hand, the totality of what is written under the signature of Fernando Pessoa does not fall under the term of orthonym, only that which he envisioned to regroup under the title of *Cancioneiro*; and on the other hand, this *Cancioneiro* alone will be included in the *Fictions of the Interlude*, next to the works of Reis, Campos, and Caeiro for poetry and Soares for prose. Nothing, however, will be definitively laid down, since Pessoa will die without his projects being carried out.

In considering the quite mysterious name Pessoa envisioned for the collection, *Fictions of the Interlude*, we notice he combines the notion of fiction, which has occupied us at length, with that of the interlude, which evokes the interval, the opening, the interim, very present in several fields of his activity – poem, prose, politics. The awareness of the poet was to belong to a time "between times": to a period in which it came to him to assure a passage between a certain state of a ruined, saturated, discredited metaphysics and a new metaphysical age to which the poet does not have the key, but to which he has the responsibility of ensuring it remains a possible figure. Such, it seems, is the meaning of this "interlude", where the heteronyms would have been the actors, or more precisely, major "fictions". The heteronyms would present an interlude for the theatre where metaphysics and poetry, in a perilous moment of their conjoined history, face off.

Although indeed, in appearance, due to the death of the poet, the non-edited final form of this poetic ensemble may seem homogeneous to the interruption which the "interlude" represents. The poetic heteronymy is the source for defining one of the sides of the crisis: it proposes a thought internal to the poem but cannot resolve it, because its own process does not authorize or have a principle of closure. The other side, the one which would beyond its undermining by the poem present a new configuration of metaphysics, remains incomplete, open, and exposed.

In this analysis of the genesis of the names, a conviction has emerged: once the orthonymy discerns a specific grouping of the poems – namely the *Cancioneiro* – the label of orthonym will not apply itself "in general" to the ensemble of that which in the oeuvre will be exterior or foreign to the heteronymy. Thus, the orthonymy cannot be identified as the opposite or underbelly of the poetic heteronymy; it designates, on the contrary, the singularity of certain poems that write themselves, make themselves, under this name. The question of what attests to this singularity appears once: by orthonymy, we no longer mean all that has been written under the name Fernando Pessoa, but that which writes itself under this name and so splinters the name in two, splitting it and distributing it into a "case" of orthonymy and an ensemble which is not.

### The allure of the orthonymous poems
The proper name of the poet is put into question in the heteronymy; it finds itself "fictioned", and the orthonymous poet answers under this "legal" name of a singular oeuvre. This Fernando Pessoa is a poet in the middle of four others.

He is an amongst-the-others and he is no position to be the creator of any of them.

The existence of the orthonym provokes a *mise-en-abime* of the figure of the author which is of an extraordinary power and radicality. The orthonymy, far from being the opposite of the heteronymy, is, in a way, a kind of intensified heteronymy, even, a heteronymy "squared": the fiction of a different poet can even present itself under the guise of the identical. This is the only way the heteronymy finds itself constituted as a consistent multiplicity. It is because there exists an orthonym amongst the four poets that the heteronymy is not reduced to a collection of false names hiding that of the author, but is capable of radically displacing any name of the author. It is not the multiplicity of names that establishes the heteronymy but the real possibility of pulling these names from the void. And yet, the orthonymy "cuts" the heteronymy in inscribing to it an empty double point: where we find Fernando Pessoa's name, he is nowhere to be found; and where the names can be found, one finds in any case the poets. In the heteronymy the name of the poet "makes" the poem, as was noted by the *Bibliographic table*, albeit in passing, and seeming not to really think it possible. Fictitious, the name of the poet is an integral part of the oeuvre, it inaugurates it; and its "non-existent person" carries it.

Thus the name of the orthonym is that which, investing in the proper name of the author, crosses it out as the name of an author, giving to the family name the status of a simple name, amongst three other chance names (the "other" names) which are equal to it. Ontologically, what the orthonymy thus exhibits, starting from the invention of Fernando Pessoa-himself, is the fictitious character of being and the original mark in him of non-being. The orthonym, as one of his poems declares, "is a being which is pure nothingness / And needs nothing". His poem will be the oeuvre of someone who "simply wants to take form / From the nothingness which surrounds his being".

> Which is the being that subsists
> Behind these apparent forms,
> The wave which consists of nothing
> The river which is only a passage?

asks a poem from the *Cancioneiro* (*The river that passes endures...*) Appearing in reaction to the oeuvre of the Keeper, the orthonym contests it in an underground manner: he attests, by the unique mixture of being and non-being which makes up his fictitious being, the maintenance within the heteronymy of the existence of the non-existent.

All of his poems strive to uncover the marks of non-being in being at the same time they attempt to determine the almost ungraspable being of thought which tracks this overlap or its traces.

In the same manner that he leaves the infinite, Caeiro leaves non-being. But, if Nature is "parts without a whole", what is there of the void in the real? Are not all the "things" of Caeiro woven from inconsistency and the void? Is not each thing, in truth, what a poem of the orthonym names a "no thing", which is to say, not completely canceled out by its proper being, but carrying in it non-being? What is it about non-being if it is definitively equal to being? And how can the poem configure such a being of non-being and such non-being of being? These questions torment the orthonymous poet, or rather provoke him (hesitating, sinuous, ambiguous) at the heart of the quartet.

What opens up the free reign of the poem in his work is no longer the will to destroy the self-interiority of thought in order to conform it to the self-exteriority of the world. This was the problem of the Keeper. It is also, albeit in a different manner, that of Campos. In the work of the orthonym, however, the exterior world is from then on entirely interior to thought. This initial interiority of the world nourishes within it a kind of hypertrophy and, above all, a hyper-excitability of thought: a nothing – a breath, a breeze, a cloud, a trill – emotionally moves it and orients it.

Forcing themselves to grasp a conjoined being of non-being and being, most of the orthonymous poems constantly divide themselves becoming, during the course of their development, "two". The orthonymous poet is equally the one who supports a split figure. Because indeed in his case, two Fernando Pessoas exist. The figure of the Two is omnipresent and matrixial in his poems. Non-being, for this poet, is no more the negation of being than the orthonym is the underside of the heteronymy. This duality of being and non-being does not employ itself according to a negative dialectic, but via the production of a fourfold seal. Non-being is apprehended by him through four figures: the seal of the void in the real; the seal of nothingness in the thought that thinks it; the seal of the nothing in the being of the poet; the seal of fiction in the poetic ontology.

And perhaps, we will find under each of these seals, established via a new link, the respective figures of Campos, Reis, Caeiro, and Fernando Pessoa-himself.

## Between being and non-being

The poem *"Oblique Rain"* occupies a founding place in the orthonymous poetry. All the more so in that it was decided as such during an initial hesitation of attribution that merits commentary: Pessoa had first thought to attribute this poem to Campos in the framework of an "intersectionist" publication project, which he will later disavow. This sudden back and forth between Campos and Fernando Pessoa-himself bears the trace of the abrupt mutation in the work of Pessoa at the end of the great crisis of 1915-1916. From the point when he starts taking the heteronymous apparition seriously in no longer attributing importance to anything but that which at the least traverses a breath of metaphysical grandeur, *"Oblique Rain"* will stop being, in his eyes, a formalist fantasy inspired by the cubist revolution and will affirm itself as powerful and dizzying poem about the vanishing being of non-being. Its author, at the same time, takes back up the lone name who could have written it. And Campos, once he is discharged of the false position of author, was charged with explaining to what degree this poem was a revelation of the most profound identity of Fernando Pessoa-himself. Here is his commentary meant for the *Family discussion*:

> *"Oblique Rain"* has no resemblance whatsoever with a poem of my master Caeiro – except for a certain recti-linearity of rhythmic movement. But Fernando Pessoa was incapable of ripping away these extraordinary poems from his interior world if he had not known Caeiro. In the moments that follow his meeting with

Caeiro, he received the spiritual impulse which produced these poems. [...] And what is the most admirable in the oeuvre of Fernando Pessoa is this ensemble of six poems, this *"Oblique Rain"*. [...] Moreover, there will be nothing which is more truly and intimately Fernando Pessoa. [...] Fernando Pessoa makes, in these poems, the veritable photography of his soul. In one moment, in one unique moment, he succeeds in having an individuality, that he never had previously, and which he did not know by himself how to become. Long live my master Caeiro! (*Pessoa por conhecer*, t. II, p. 413.)

An ensemble composed, as Campos underlines, of six distinct poems, "Oblique Rain" proceeds in its pursuit of being and non being via subtle variations all starting from the same abstract construction. In fact, this poem strives to grasp in which way, if there is being and non-being and if non-being exists within being, thought can, in its own manner open itself up to this splitting: in such a way it can "free itself within both of them". The first three poems differ in a very slight manner, but all share the trait of being built on successive transparencies: an imaginary reflection of a port gliding in the landscape composed of trees and flowers in the sun; a vision of a church appearing under a curtain of rain; the apparition of the Great Sphinx of Egypt in the fabric of the paper on which the poem is written. Under successive veils of water, rain, and paper, being allows itself be apprehended in the guise of non-being that inhabits it.

Following the lead of what happens in a good number of poems from the *Cancioneiro*, the initial situation of each one of these figures is that of an awakened dream: a state between sleep and dreaming, propitious to swerving into the unreal. This pensive indecision of reverie allows the poem to let precariousness, the unstable fluidity of being, flourish: the imaginary reflection of a port appearing within the interior vision of the sunlit landscape traverses and mixes with it, undoing its unity and destabilizing its appearance. Great ships on dreamed up waters tack their masts amongst the silhouettes of old trees. Imperceptibly, the imaginary port overcomes the landscape and converts all things from the real world into elements from its kingdom of fantasy. It is soon impossible to tell whether what the poem sees is a path or a dock, if the ships come and go between the trees in the sun, or if these trees reflect each other in what would be the water of a port. Nothing any longer allows us to distinguish between the initial sunlit vision and the dreamed up maritime landscape. Only their transmutability can be apprehended, equally woven from being and non-being.

Moreover, a theatrical act – an abrupt balance intervenes – according to a schema which will repeat itself in all the following variations: the moving image of the port, becoming prevalent, suddenly becomes immobile, deploying a vast liquid transparency under which, "like an immense print that finds itself opened up", the initial landscape reappears. The being of landscape acquires its greatest clarity in the transparency of its "non-being", the immobile waters of the port. In turn, the non-being of the dreamed port is "fixed", or rendered apparent, by the engraving it leaves of itself at the bottom of the clear water. Thus, the real in a way finds itself "engraved" by being once non-being is co-present with it, whereas this non-being exists only when it is generated by being, attached to being, interior to it. It is via the unheard-of interweaving of these images that the poem is capable of constructing here for the very first time the figure of the seal of the void in the real.

The non-being that the dream of the imaginary port introduced to the sunlit landscape showed a power equal to being, but this power proper to non-being does not cancel out being. It has simply woven their reciprocal rearranging, revealing a union that the poem was able to render visible during the course of its own translations and shifts between two images.

However, barely stabilized, the situation takes on a new development: "the shadow of a ship, older than the port" *between* the dream of the port and vision of the landscape, "nearing me, profoundly penetrating in me, / And passing *across the other side* of my soul". What is this vessel of which the poem only lets us glimpse an uncertain shadow? What to make of this shadowy ship which, floating between the images of being and non-being, passes across to the other side of the poet's soul? Is it not the image of non-being present in thought itself, which allows it to slide between being and non-being, navigating between one and the other, the movement of the path which separates them? The poem here would this time present the necessary mark of nothingness in thought which thinks non-being.

The two variations which follow reiterate a very similar journey demonstrating the virtuosity of the orthonym to play with his materials. From the interior of a rainy day appears the phantasmagoria of an illuminated church: the vision of this imaginary place acquires such a degree of influence that it annexes the rain, which from that instant appears to fall inside the church amidst the chants between the choirs; like the vessel, an automobile, identified by the noise of its motor, emerges from both the rainy landscape and the church mass, arriving at its most intense moment traverses this double scene. This evokes the exercise of "simple hallucination" by Rimbaud (*A season in hell*: "I saw quite frankly a mosque in the place of a factory, a school of drums made by angels, carriages on the streets of heaven, a living-room at the end of a lake.") to the extent the fragment of the poem this time highlights the copulative "is" of the analogy. Then, this whole chimera stops in the exact instant the rain stops falling. When the veil of rain disappears, through which being attached to non-being became visible, all vision finds itself just as quickly abolished. Being thus appears only under the conditions of being what it is not.

"Equivalences" and "analogies" of the orthonym materialize the translation which operates between being and non-being. All the figures of thought which weave his poems are figures of indiscernibility between being and non-being:

> Yes, everything is analogy, equivalence.
> The wind which passes, this cold night,
> [..] are *other things* than wind and night—
> Dreams of Being and Thought.

> ("I hear the wind pass in the night"[12])

[12] Fernando Pessoa, *Cancioneiro*, poèmes 1911-1935, translation from French by Michel Chandeigne and Patrick Quillier, in collaboration with Maria Antonia Câmara Manuel and Liberto Cruz, with the participation of Lucien Kebren and Maria Teresa Leitão, and a preface by Robert Bréchon, Paris, Christian Bourgois, 1988: 86.

We understand by the light of these lines with what force Pessoa "non-exists" when Caeiro appears. The Keeper, hostile to the idea that Nature can express or signify anything whatsoever, that a thing can be something other than a thing, will not know how to agree with this declaration of the orthonymous poetics. But the orthonym, contrary to Reis and Campos, is not a disciple of Caeiro. Fernando Pessoa-himself is the one who resists Caeiro's anti-expressive poetic revolution and manifests, in the name of the existence of non-being, an insistent objection.

The third variation inscribes in the poem the obliquity of which its enigmatic title claims to be a representative. From the Great Sphinx, barely inferred by the watermark of the paper on which the poet writes, arises an overpowering Egypt. First, the cadaver of King Kheops, brutally thrown onto the paper; then, entering into an image which again takes up the motif of the ship, the immense Nile river and its gloating vessels. Its waters flow according to the quite curious notation of the poem, "between the gazes" of the poet and the dead king, and more precisely as a consequence, "on a diffuse diagonal / Between me and what I think". This diagonal along which the river flows sketches an abstract site where being and non-being articulate themselves and blend the present and the dreamed. It is the ridgeline of their reversible indistinctness. This obliquity of the diagonal elucidates the title of the poem: oblique is the singular operation by which the poem captures under certain conditions the non-dialectical apparitions/disappearances of being and non-being.

The following variation subtlety complicates the walk of a group of young girls in the light of a great sun and the noisy radiance of a nocturnal circus. But

> Suddenly, someone shakes like in a sieve, this double hour
> And confused, the dust of the two realities falls
> On my hands covered with drawings of ports, [...]
> Black and white gold dust on my fingers.

The entanglement of being and non-being undoes itself revealing that being and non-being exist in two different forms even though the real is made up of singular "black and white gold" dust in which the impression of gold wins out over the dichotomy of black and white. The one who undoes the entanglement of being and non-being is anonymous and indistinct: "someone" himself bearing the mark of nothing. The beauty of this scene is found in the forceful emergence, under the guise of a conjurer, of the orthonym as magician.

Yet still more complex is the last part of the poem. "Analogy" indeed perfects itself by the incredible multiplication of successive shifts around which the poem proceeds. It is true that it no longer works starting from two initial elements, as was the case in the preceding parts, but from four: one part being the image of an orchestra conductor accompanied by his "sad and languid music"; one part being that of child's ball, presenting in its turn on one of its sides "the slide of a green dog" and on the other, "a blue horse galloping under a yellow jockey". Yellow jockey, green dog, blue horse, black orchestra conductor, sad music, but also theatre and garden, skillfully exchange their places. In this new apparatus, a separate identity of being and non-being again becomes nearly impossible.

When the music stops, the orchestra conductor briefly fuses with the characters represented on the ball; he confuses himself with the yellow jockey, "turning (himself) black", and finds himself perched on the blue horse; then the ball reappears one final time on the head of the musician before disappearing, guided by invisible hands behind his back.

Campos, in his commentary on *"Oblique Rain"*, did not miss the chance to direct attention towards the fact that in this poem, "the state of the soul is simultaneously two"; the objective and the subjective, which are separated, here join together, and yet remain nonetheless separate; and "the real and the unreal blur (together) and yet still remain distinct". According to him, the poem deals with the dual principle itself: in particular of the "Two" of the object and subject which organize the whole metaphysical apparatus. We should also note, however, that the orthonym introduces a new dualism which results from the instability and inextricability of being and non-being and of the splitting of any thought consecrated to it. Thus the question of non-being extremely complicates the critique of dualism that Caeiro maintains.

What is proposed here will be confirmed but also nuanced via a new reading of "She sings, poor harvester..."

### A thought of the Two

This poem is centered on thought. Its apparent occasion is the analogy of a song by a woman busy harvesting, which this poet grasps as an ideal of his thought. The song is the veil of non-being behind which a being lets itself be glimpsed. The poem first of all renders the melody visible:

it names the "curves" of the voice, evokes the "sweet fabric of sound that it weaves", describes it "undulating" in the air.

"Believing herself to be happy, perhaps", and singing "as if in order to sing, she had other reasons than life", the harvester captures the attention of the poet by the unconscious, or better, in-awareness of herself where she is located. She inspires in him the wish of possessing this same unconscious, if it could be one which was simultaneously a knowing unconscious, one aware of its unconsciousness:

> Have your merry unconscious
> And the awareness of it!

The initial figure of the harvester at her work splits and gives birth to a second figure, the orthonym haunted by the desire to juxtapose the self-unawareness of the singer with his own awareness. If this figure can divide itself in such a manner, it is because there was an invisible rift located in it perceptible in what the poet calls the "anonymous and joyous widowhood" of the song. This simple country worker, inhabited by a void that she herself does not suspect, but which her song unveils, becomes a character for metaphysics. This transformation has never been more perceptible than when we compare the poem to its genuine source, which is less the scene of a Portuguese countryside than a poem of the English poet, Wordsworth. António Feijó, during a conference in Paris in 1996, announced that this poem was the re-writing by Pessoa of the famous English poem: "The Solitary Reaper". A re-writing that is at the same time a critique. This process of re-writing – it seems fair for me to call it an "un-writing" – largely found in the work of Caeiro, thus also finds itself in the work of the orthonym. Each one of these four poets probably found in romantic English poetry a major subtext to which all the heteronymous poetry is the critique "in poems".

### Between consciousness and unconsciousness

The orthonym analyzes in the seduction of the song of the harvester the delights of the unawareness of self, analogon of the necessary conformation of his own thought to nothingness. Unawareness, as exteriority in the work of Caeiro, is in his eyes the norm of thought: for a thought that is not a knowing-thought, a thought of science. Sadness, gently present in the inflections of the song, is in its turn constituted from that which the desire of the poet brushes up against: the impossibility of unawareness to be aware of itself. The poem melancholically closes with the feeling of an impossible ideal briefly accomplished.

Accomplished via the intersection and recognition of the metaphysical figure offered up in the song of an anonymous woman who is not herself aware of what her song suggests.

The orthonymous poem is the "faint shadow" of this happy and unstable ensemble composed by the song, fields, and sky. It elusively disposes non-being of this versatile being in order then for this shadow as well to be able to pass and dissolve itself.

The "faint shadow" is a possible name of non-being as the orthonym grasps it: it is actually attached to being, but distinct from it like a shadow from its silhouette; it is not the double, nor the reflection, nor the reverse side of being; it is without being proper and nevertheless correlated to each existence; it is unique like the thing, but is not one; it proceeds from a presence of which it is not the negation, but evidence of its hollowing out.

Thus the orthonym returns in another poem about desire to establish poetic thought in the field of a conscious unconsciousness. He accentuates the always involuntary character of thought, which renders it identical to the blossoming of a flower. This includes the part which we call "consciousness", where free-will has no place. Thought exists independently of us more than we believe:

> If the flower blooms without wanting to,
> It is indeed without wanting to that we think.
> What in it is blooming
> Is for us to have consciousness.

("I don't know how to really be sad…", *Cancioneiro*, p. 46)

### Far from me in me I exist

In the orthonymous poems, the inconsistency of any unity, the absence of any figure of the One, does not exchange itself in the diverse and multiple, but within the split and the Two.

The fictitious existence of Fernando Pessoa-himself is in itself a denial of any figure of the One, since the orthonym bears the Two of a name divided by fiction. Pessoa-himself is a sort of inscription or immediate materialization interior to the heteronymy from which the One does not exist.

A poem, "The child played", retraces as quasi-primitive experience of splitting and analyzes what plays itself out in the emergence of a "Two". A young boy busy playing with a cart discovers there exists two beings in him and not just one. He first names them: the "one who plays", and "the one who knows it". This divided child is from then on capable of reaching what the couple of the harvester and the poet listening to her sing were not: he identifies in himself the obscure co-existence of a figure of unconsciousness and a figure of consciousness. Because it is in him that we find present the one who plays and sees himself playing and the one who is in the middle of gazing at the one who plays. This latter one, which the poet calls "the other boy", "has neither hands nor feet". He is not properly speaking a child, because he does not have a mother or brothers either. Nor is he a father or guardian, nor "body", nor friend of the one who discovers he is "two". If he were any of these, there would be three rather than two: the three resulting from the one added to the two in which the child split; or the three coming from a third reuniting and containing the two others. And yet the child and the poem maintain that here there is only a Two and not a One. The one who stands "behind" the child, when the child turns around, teaches him that he is not himself this "one" he believes to be, since, immediately as he turns around, the one who was standing there vanishes. The second boy exists exactly at the same point as the first: he is thus made from nothing other than from a "without being"; he is the fluttering between being and non-being. And, nevertheless, he is the key of the real, of the real of being as well of the real of thought. The child says of him:

Here in this place he has a soul,
He sees me without seeing:
The small cart
Begins to appear.

("The child played")

Under his auspice, the poem ends in jubilation. His gaze pulls the being away from the toy to withdraw from where he stood and to make appearance sparkle. The child "frees himself" in the Two, according to the equation from *"Oblique Rain"*. Moreover, then the real comes to him like a wonderful surprise.

## Return of the heteronymy concerning the orthonym

The refusal of the One presents itself as well in the work of this poet as a denial of the Self and thus as a mode of consciousness.

If he utters with violence (in the poem "I am an escapist…", *Cancioneiro*, p. 134):

To be one, is a prison,

it is because he can declare with the most extreme preciseness regarding "himself", the fictitious Pessoa:

To be me is not to be.

There are numerous orthonymous poems which describe the dissolution of any personal identity within an obscure multiplicity. Within one of them, within an image of a nightmare, the poet describes the identical crowd of "his" others tumbling down an immense staircase:

> Ah, how horrible a resemblance they have!
> They are even a multiple which is not aware of itself.
> I watch them. All of them I am, without being any of them.

> ("The child that I was cries on the street", *Cancioneiro*, p. 179)

The horror here is not caused by alterity, but by resemblance: in the orthonymy, multiplicity is repetition of the same and not the proliferation of the diverse. This singularity of the orthonym makes itself perceptible as well in the poem which shows the sufferance of soul scattered into pieces: "soul fragments", debris of being and non-being. The orthonym underlines the proof of being by one's self "many people", of not being able to "feel with a lone soul", of having lost all certitude of possessing one's own unique soul. There where Campos bemoans not having ownership of all places and things, Fernando Pessoa complains of being too capable of this:

> Not having a home, is it!
> No relaxation and no attachments, that's it!
> But, I, because I possess so many souls,
> I am not even capable of possessing my own.

> ("I would have loved, really...", *Cancioneiro*, p. 119)

The orthonym in a sense supports the entire heteronymy. He is aware of all the fictions and of the constant non-existence of self they induce. Even in his fictitious persona, the orthonym is in pursuit of the throes of non-being. He either feels great pain or a kind of demiurgic pride, for example in this poem which demands, not without an ironic height, as a divine trait, the inconsistent multiplicity of his being:

The one who believes to be himself is in error,
Me, I am various, and do not belong to myself.
   [...]
God possesses a mode of being various,
Various are the modes from which I am made.
Thus, of God, I am the imitator,
Because, once he created what is,
He will take away infinity from it
And even unity.

("I leave it to the blind and deaf...", *Cancioneiro*, p. 124-125)

## The audible smile of leaves

If the smile of leaves lets itself strangely be heard and not seen, it is because the material of the orthonym's poems, contrary to those of the Keeper, is not the visible: for him, "everything is heard, nothing is seen". And it is most often under the aspect of the dreamed-thing, of the invisible, or the poorly visible, but also via music and all the near or distant sounds, that most of the poems grasp being in its connection with non-being.

Music and sounds, by the temporal succession they generate, allow Fernando Pessoa to open the poem up to the temporality of splitting, of the emergence of this omnipresent "two" by which he establishes the non-existence of any "One". We agree to name this trait in his work as "two", or dual, and not "double". This orthonymous "Two" does not juxtapose being and non-being as the inside and outside, nor does it generate one by the negation of the other; it affirms the coextensivity of both as well as the time and the place, all of which the poem must construct. The shadow of the ship, the diagonal of the river, the spiral of a song are both in time and space:

mobile figures of a sliding, flowing, winding of being and non-being. The time of the orthonymous poem is entirely inferred from the effort to decompose in thought the versatile unstable entanglement of being and non-being. Thus, we are here dealing with a temporality rather than a time, of a temporality necessary for the capture and untangling of this Two.

## Being is a fiction

The subjective complication of this poetry is extreme. It explores without tiring the undividable "duality" of being and non-being. Contrary to what the poem of the Keeper constantly exposes, for Fernando Pessoa being is never exactly what it seems to be. Each thing is sealed with non-being and can, as a consequence, be understood as "no-thing".

### If all that exists is a lie...

In a very surprising poem, he deliberately hijacks the image of the sunflower which we know constitutes one of the images on the blazon of Caeiro ("My gaze is as clear as a sunflower"). In the middle of the yellow petals of non-being, the orthonymous sunflower bears the dark heart of nothingness:

> Sunflower to the illusory fondness
> Around the silent center
> It speaks, yellow, stupefied
> By the dark center which is everything

> ("I still remain, like a stupor...", *Cancioneiro*, p. 144)

Still pondering non-being, the void, nothing, and nothingness, Fernando Pessoa is, of the four poets, the most fiercely exposed to nihilism. Two lines condense this nihilism into a syllogism which offers itself up at times as a fault and at times as a powerful affirmation:

> If all that exists is a lie
> Lying is all that exists.

("If all that exists...", *Cancioneiro*, p. 153)

This inclination makes a profoundly "out-of-work" figure out of him, in the literal sense; namely he is always on the verge of being without an oeuvre – to the extent that his oeuvre strives to name that which hesitates between existence and nothingness. Its production is as discontinuous and delay-laden as the production of the Keeper is articulated and demonstrative. Any orthonymous poem takes place in an "interval between being and non-being". It exists

> Only by the example of such dust:
> Visible when the wind rustles them
> They live from being shown

("Every being that I am...", *Cancioneiro*, p. 185)

This between-two of the poem is linked, as *"Oblique Rain"* already maintains, to this existence in the work of the orthonym of "another side" which being and thought would have to share:

> Everything is on the other side,
> In what there is, and in what I think.

("I contemplate what I do not see...", *Cancioneiro*, p. 189)

In order to discover this "other side", thought first strives to construct a quite improbable location outside the field of vision. The orthonym indicates, marking his distance from the Keeper, "I contemplate, *what I do not see*." This search gives most of his poems an extraordinarily tortuous and fleeting path:

> Between the world and nothingness
> I lost myself.

> ("I slept. I dreamt.")

This sudden erratic straying instills a pocket of darkness. The poem collapses into a cul-de-sac or inflicts upon itself a brutal interruption. Light is thus very fragile to it, "tiny" and nearly absent:

> The entire being that I am is nothing more than a ruin
> In the inside of which a tiny light
> Which tells me it's me – and I think about it without end –
> Obscure leads me.

> ("The entire being that I am...", *Cancioneiro*, p. 185)

Just as firmly as Caeiro, Fernando Pessoa-himself is established in the Parmenidean certainty according to which "the same are being and thought". But his peculiar manner of affirming it is interior to his vision of thought as unconsciousness:

> That which exists merges
> With what I am and sleep.

Whereas as a radical nihilism convinces him that

> From nothing, we take away nothing
> To nothing, we give nothing.

> ("If all that exists...", *Cancioneiro*, p. 153)

The power of non-being is nevertheless a power of affirmation:

> In no case is the immense sky
> Missing to the agitated branch.

## The songs (Les chants)

When one of these orthonymous poems is able to pin down to the point of nothing a being of non-being, its allure becomes that of a free and airy song. It is precisely these sorts of poems that justify the curious title of *Cancioneiro* under which Pessoa had wanted to organize his orthonymous poems. Three of them, respectively titled, "My lines, are my transcribed dreams"; "Yes, a song rises in the night"; "At the core of my thought, a song has got a hold of my place of sleep" – have quite a singular beauty and clarity. Their analysis renders possible seeing what distinguishes these "songs" amongst the orthonymous poems.

First of all, paradoxically, an orthonymous song is an anonymous song. Contrary to what happens in lyricism, no personal voice is identifiable. This anonymity is born from the statement of any significant figure, according to four rules that the first of these poems utters in the form of a charade:

> What we have known, we lose.
> What we think, we have already been.
> We only keep what we have given.
> The main thing consists in being what we are not.

Knowledge is vain, thought is caught within the non-being of what it apprehends, what could be conserved is what has been dispersed in the gift.

The orthonym "sings to belong to itself", but its song is the epitome of depersonalization.

Secondly, the poet does not hear what he sings. He has no knowledge or awareness of it until someone else hears it and understands it. "Feelings? It's up to the reader to feel!" The mocking "fall" of *This-here* (*Ceci*) says quite well, via the form of irony, that the freedom of the poet has a condition: the poem, to be complete, must meet a reader, a reader who, all kidding aside, is not useless. Because it is the reader who effectuates, between being and non-being, the consistency of the poem, and concludes the movement of thought. That "everything depends on what has no existence" is indeed the re-iterated certitude of the orthonymous poet. Non-being is the mark of being and not the opposite.

When he gets carried away by nihilism, the orthonym summons a god who guarantees that the pendulum does not come to a halt on the side of nothingness, but of being and non-being, it continues to oscillate without end. A god in the absence of chance, in sum:

> Mom, would there not be
> A god in order to prevent everything from becoming vain,
> Another world where all of this continues to exist?

asks "The veil of tears does not make you blind" (*Cancioneiro*, p. 217) When the song makes itself the direct presence of music (trills from a flute, chiming from a church bell, song of the harvester, the wear or immense sound of the wind), it is capable of composing the mobile figure of that which is "merely distance / Or which will never have existence."

The orthonym stubbornly maintains, against the thought of things which is that of the Keeper, the ontological objection of non-being. The Keeper and the Fictioneer are not master and disciple: their encounter is that of a poet without metaphysics and that of a poet deprived of philosophy. If the latter one bears the "correct" name, it is no doubt because he is the one who, contrary to Caeiro, wants to make exist in the poem a figure of non-being, to which philosophy has never stopped identifying the most severe ontological difficulties.

### "Fictioneering" is the business of the poet

"Fingidor": compulsive liar, cheater, faker...? It is difficult to encounter in French a suitable substitute for translating this, which, according to the orthonym, essentially describes the poet. Trick and fiction are the best approximations in their distance from the question of truth. We should remember moreover that Pessoa named the volume around which he envisioned the construction of the heteronymy *Fictions of the Interlude*. In order to translate: "O poeta e um fingidor", it is acceptable in these conditions to propose: "The poet fictioneers." Thus highlighting that the strongest discovery of the orthonym is that everything that touches being comes from fiction. What his poem transmits – what there was (maybe) of being – transmits itself via a fiction in which being is absented but in which its traces of existence are conserved. The being of being can only be grasped through the bias of this fictional staging, and single-handedly reproduces the seal of being and non-being. This fiction is thus not a lie. It is a construction that reveals that the site of being is not truth. The orthonym needs this in order to attest and inscribe the non-coincidence of the being of being and the being of a truth.

The following minuscule poem delivers this "minimal" equation:

> Cramped, tranquil, lamp.
> Illuminating you and enlightening me
> Oscillating *between who I am and who you are.*

(Cancioneiro, p. 159)

Here we are dealing with a kind of *haikai* focused on the beat between being and non-being. There is first of all a turned off lamp – in the middle of becoming illuminated. The light thus exists at the same time as the dark which had existed before the light emerges. The poem travels so fast that it is almost capable of showing at the same time what there is and is not. Someone is present, anonymous, indistinct, as is often the case in the work of the orthonym. From him, nothing more exists than the gesture of lighting the lamp. His identity is the oscillation between a new apparition introduced by the "who I am" and the lamp, which the poem addresses itself and which finds itself symmetrically identified by a "who you are". Once more, the poem moves quickly by the concentrated effect of the pronouns. This rapidity forces a third element to emerge: the poet on the verge of writing, raising his hand to allow the light to shine through. But do the hand that illuminates and the hand that writes fuse together? The primary presence only exists as an eclipse between the poet and the object while another presence reveals itself, that of the reader, around which the admirable miniature closes itself.

The poem, "Autopsychography", has often been commented on because it is a sort of manifestation of this vision of the poet as "fictioneer". The one who has staged "two sufferings" – the one who felt it (perhaps) and the one who feels it via the delay of the poem – forces an unexpected third term to surface: the suffering of which the readers are not victim, but in reading the poem nonetheless feel – a pain which is nothing other in its own right than the non-being of the suffering of the poet. And which was already woven in part from non-being by the fictional staging in the poem. Whatever suffering the poem creates in the reader, this suffering will be neither that which the poet felt, nor that which he inscribed in the poem. And yet, all this is done in order to up the ante of simulation: it will be its own suffering which will find itself put on display. Only a double "fictioning" is susceptible of transcribing being from non-being and non-being from being. And this invention alone attests that the being which the poem alone is capable of capturing, so precarious, evanescent, however well kept, is nonetheless never nothing or indifferent.

## The just poem

The poem *She came elegant, in a hurry…* – in which we can find an un-writing of the famous poem by Baudelaire, "À une passante" (*To a passerby*) – is a striking example of the method of orthonymous fictioneering. Two lines suffice in order for a woman in the middle of the crowd at the street corner to surface. Two more lines and the "proper poem" of this encounter proclaims to be made. But, in the following four lines, the contents of what the poem should be find themselves prescribed differently. The just poem – the poem says – would not speak of this woman. It would not describe her at all, nor would recount

> [...] how, woman child,
> She turns on the angle of this
> Street which is the eternal angle...

(OP[13], pp. 806-807)

The just poem would be the one which would know how not to speak of the glimpsed woman nor of the regret of her disappearance, but of things quite distanced from the encounter and its site, such as the waves and the sea. The just poem would know how to compose and transmit a fictitious suffering in resorting to other shifting ingredients.

The orthonymous figure of thought takes shape here in a decisive manner and whose analogy is an approximate name. When this poet declares that the "trees, wind, the night", "are something other than they are", it is not that he renders Nature an expressivity nor that he strives to endow it with meaning. For him, it is about capturing how *each* thing is also at the same time *another thing* – being *and* non-being from *within itself.* Describing the encounter itself means necessarily to see what it no longer is, which is equal to dissolving or losing it. Whereas the sea and the waves can carry not only the regret of the loss of the glimpsed woman, but also the fading being of the

---

[13] Cf. p. 43. N. 1.

encounter. The non-being interior to the thing opens up to the expressivity, which is not that of the thing itself, but that of another thing. This is the reason that only the "just poem", which is to say, the one capable of recomposing in the presentation from a configuration entirely of fictitious being and non-being the being that was, has some chance of resuscitating the real suffering: the memory of the "cruel angle".

## The clinamen of the poem

The "proper poem" thus writes itself in the denial of what it writes; it takes the place of the poem which would not be made, but also the existence of which he makes allusion. By this method, he is not absolutely assured a poem ever resuscitates the cruel angle: the poem does not exclude that a memory obtained by such a means can be either that of the woman or that "of the water". It does not do away with the possibility of a refusal of the real with the support of non-being which fiction has at its disposal.

One should indeed bet some other singular force in order for the happy scheme of this singular expressivity to organize itself. In order for analogy to not be reduced to an artificial and vague rapprochement, in order for it to be a figure of thought which captures the real, the constant sliding between being and non-being must not stop at the point of non-being. One must bear the risk of a poetic fiction in which a fictitious non-being "stumbles across" a being that has already disappeared, thus reconstructing the being of the thing. This movement of the risky fall and directed attraction irresistibly evokes the *clinamen*.

In the poem about the passerby, by a brilliant round of sleight of hand, the existing poem is not the "just poem" stipulated in the poem, but a poem speaking about what would make up the "just poem", partly writing it and partly effacing it. But it is indeed this poem here, prescribing the poem without being it itself, which captures the real of the encounter. It is itself caught in the law of the orthonym: poem of the "just poem", it can only be as such under the condition of being other than its being. This is why the poem about the "just poem" is also a poem about the figure of the encounter: this one, the non-being of fiction records the flapping of the wings of a being "soaring off other" in its non-being.

The entirety of this oeuvre conceives itself as a "vain cadastre of being". Depicting itself as Pessoa-Prometheus, making from his being a torch to light from his own nothingness the anguishing duplicity of the "no-thing", the poet sums up his vocation in these poignant words:

> I have failed.
> Finally! I have succeeded in being who I am,
> Already no-thing, in this old woods in which
> I shall, since I only have value in offering myself up,
> Easily start a fire from a spark
>
> ("I have failed...", *Cancioneiro*, p. 201)

The orthonymous poet is a Hamlet whose dreamy madness is wanting at the same time to be *and* not be.

# 6
# Dissolving the figure of the gods

Ricardo Reis, the first disciple of Caeiro, only exists on March 8, 1914 in the state of a poet without an oeuvre. The character appears, a unique case amongst the four, before any poem. In part, this reason certainly comes from his extreme proximity with Caeiro; another reason arises from the fact that he deploys his aesthetic in critical reaction to the oeuvre of Campos. Thus, his poetic existence is largely dependent on the existence of their works.

This poet acutely analyses the contingency of existence and the world which infers itself from the thought of the Keeper. From the thought of things where Caeiro is the calm master, the poetry of Reis is, in some manner, the affect. The singular site of his poetry is the meditation on the meaninglessness of existence once the being of the universe finds itself reduced to the pure multiple of things. Compared to the fearlessness of the sunflower-gaze of Caeiro, this torment and the inflictions it imposes to thought are felt in these lines:

> I love what I see, because I will cease
> One day or another from seeing it

> ("I love what I see…", OP, p. 171)

Or again here:

> I hate what I don't see
>
> ("I do not interrogate the anonymous future...", OP, p. 148)

Reis finds himself caught between the fascination he has for the onto-poetic innovation held by the Keeper and the impossibility from where he is standing to repeat, and sometimes even accept, the thought-poem. The poignant density of Reis' poetry finds itself concealed by the anti-modernist positions taken by him. And yet, when Wallace Stevens declares that after the great poems of heaven and hell, the poems of the earth should be written, it is towards Reis that one must turn in order to find such a splendid sketch.

## Nothing inside of nothing, such is man

Reis refuses the idea that there would exist two regimes of Being. There does not exist a being of man which would differentiate itself from the being of things. Man is like things, because he is himself a thing. He is not at all an exception in the universe. Here resides the austere grandeur of this poetry, which we could say gives itself up to a de-anthropologization of ontology to the degree that it casts aside any privilege of man at the heart of Nature. His existence turns out to be just as contingent and devoid of meaning as the rest of the Universe. But, on the other hand, according to a counter-effect or by a deliberate counter-movement, this poetry is centered on man to the extent that the poetry declares him to be nothing. From Caeiro to Reis, an ontological displacement occurs, because being "nothing", and even more having to be aware of this nothing, is in excess of the "being a thing" of Caeiro. Nor is this nothing of Reis the non-being of the orthonym. It is that of death, of time, of what "is disappearing".

This heteronym is not capable of being a-subjective like Caeiro or even of sharing what he names in his own terms as "the absolute objectivism" of his master. He is tormented by the *consequences* of the thought of the Keeper: things are devoid of signification and meaning indicates for him that the universe is literally nonsensical (*insensé*). How does one live a thought where "things exists and that is it", knowing that one must in addition live without letting oneself turn away from this thought?

His poems strive to give form to a courage such that it would allow for the support of the contingency of human perception without reconstituting a transcendence nor searching to define immanence. In this way, the *Odes* divide themselves up into meditations, canvases, and maxims. Meditations about life are of a character devoid of any meaning of existence. Canvases of thought: what would the value be of what Reis names "the scruple of thought" on the balance of a crazed life? Some maxims, ultimately about courage: in order to drive out anxiety and overcome dereliction, we must conform our thought to the being of the world; in order for "acceptance to be our lone science", it should propose a wisdom.

The desire to retrace the thought the Keeper taught him concerning things, and explicitly applying them to men, animates the entirety of Reis' oeuvre. Despite the fact his own style is often tense and anguished, in reading it, we can see a strong feeling of proximity with Caeiro – much more immediately perceptible than in the case of Campos, the second disciple. So it is that Caeiro's thesis, "To be complete it is simply enough to exist", becomes, applied to man by Reis: "We lack nothing, because we are nothing." And all of our "grand appearances" are useless, because

> Nothing, in this foreign world,
> Recognizes our apparent grandeur

> ("The sea is a mourning place...")

Man bears no figure of meaning whatsoever. An integral part of the universe, he has no more meaning than the world itself. It would be good to patiently acquire this conviction, rather than ignore our lack of control regarding destiny, or what Reis magnificently names "the piles of the future". When it makes itself affirmative, this poetry reunites with the most firm Lucretian accents, "Nothing inside of nothing", such is man.

The figure of nothingness, so obsessive in the work of the orthonym, is also present in the work of Reis where it does not show itself as an aporia of thought, but as a trouble of existence: it deprives life of any peace. Because it is difficult to admit that we have all been lead "into the labile race of Being", and that

> We make no more noise amongst all that exists
> Than leaves in trees
> And the blowing of the winds

> ("Before us, through the same trees...", *Pagan Poems*, p. 166[14])

---

[14] PP= *Poèmes païens d'Alberto Caeiro* translated to French by Michel Chandeigne, Patrick Quillier, and Maria Antonia Câmara Manuel, Paris, Christian Bourgois, 1989.

Men suffer and despair about being handed over to non-sense. But it is this despair alone that oppresses them; they must understand that they are only "subject(s) of no instance"; that no power, no "exterior" instance – the word has a singular Kafkaesque resonance – no god has enslaved them.

If the poet describes existence as a "villa allocated by the gods" to man in order remove him from summer, more frequent are the painful allusions to the rowboat that only ever returns empty, to the small coin offered to the hand of a cadaver, to the boatman placed on the "occult bank" of the river of the Dead, in the darkness where one must "wander without flowers in the haunted ruin of rumors". Because the one who gazes perishes with that which he gazes, he is carried away in the disappearance of what he has seen:

> In what I looked at, in part I have remained.
> When one thing I have seen has passed, I pass as well
> Without distinguishing the memory
> Of what I have seen from what I have been
>
> ("In all that ceases…")

Against this sinking in "what is passing", which is the possible reverse of the ontology of the Keeper, the poet forms the splendid wish of suspending the "Apollonian race" from the sun, thus to become the "demented twin / of an imperishable hour". Abolishing time supposes it has no exterior or objective identity whatsoever. Such is the meaning of the suggestion: "Seize the day, because you *are* the day." The poet contrasts the business of the world with the "desire of indifference", the willingness to be nothing more than a "phlegmatic debt in the fugitive hour". He affirms his indifference to history and to the becoming of people, his disdain for any homeland, and his denial of any event.

To consent to injustice is just as difficult, but as necessary as abolishing time. Reis thus speaks of "expelling the gesture of justice", underlining the violent effort necessary in order to rip oneself away from the call to war, homeland, and life.

### Three feminine figures and love

Love suspected of being fake or a lie, love that exposes deception and sorrow and worsens the influence of death by the pain of the loss of a loved-one, love, nonetheless, should be sought out in so far as it procures a figure of withdrawal and distance. Its own precariousness, its fragility, is emblematic of what is aleatory and perishable in the world and the universe. When love exists, it is always

> as if when the kiss ends
> [...] should destroy itself, suddenly,
> Enormous, the mass of the dead world

> ("The leaf without consciousness...", OP, p. 1728)

"Leaning towards beauty / Wherever it may be", love no more sees "the branch on which it places itself" than the bird. This inclination of being towards beauty is not only indifferent to gender but humanity, and definitively indifferent to the thing which causes it, since

My love does not reside in her, but
In my love

("The bird places itself and barely sees...", PP, p. 263)

In what Reis calls love, what is sought is a certain pacified relationship to being. This is why the "final cause" of such a love is beauty, which can find itself distributed in the man or woman, but also in the fruit or flower. To love the beauty in a flower can procure a calming effect equal to, perhaps even greater than, loving a woman. This love is not necessary, it pursues no intention, and it lazily follows the slope which favors it. It is valuable only if it helps in overcoming the terror of having to conceive of oneself as thing.

Three women one after another are invoked by the poet: Neaere, Chloe, and Lydia. Are they merely names, spindly phantoms, pieces plucked from Latin literature? Or can we distinguish in them individuated figures of love as it has just been defined?

Chloe is the most fleeting of the three silhouettes. She incarnates a love hurried by death, a passion from which one should either free oneself as fast as possible or, the exact opposite, enjoy by in a kind of fit of anger trying to gain speed on the memory which it never stops from becoming at each second.

Neaere bears the name of a woman blackmailed by an ancient poet, fictitious himself, "Lygdamus" who is supposed to be the author of the first six pieces of Book III from the *Elegies* of Tibulle. As far as she is concerned, she is blond, and thus the only one who bears a physical trait.

This figure is more friendly than loving, she is like a mirror of experience through which the poet struggles to do away with the terror of death. A young girl, Neaere is in fact his "apprentice". He teaches her how to tame anxiety by adding to the conduct of his life merely "the sadness of a sigh", in remaining at the surface of thought, and in fleeing "far from men and cities" in order to feel liberated from a face-off with death.

No less than 22 poems are dedicated to Lydia, who bears the name of a very ancient province of Asia Minor. The poems no longer compose the image of a young girl, but of a woman equal to the poet with whom he speaks in complete confidence and certitude of being understood, without having to spell it out. From the roses she carries, or which are offered to her, a classical symbol of the briefness of life, the poet takes away a new teaching: these flowers live and die within the span of one day, between sunrise and sunset, in such a manner that "light is eternal to them". Let us thus reject the idea that before and after our own experience, Night surrounds us. Let us consider each life as equivalent to "a day", not in order to shorten it, but to render it exactly contemporaneous with the light of this singular day, because in this manner, it becomes eternal.

The poet shares with this woman the knowledge of contingency and of the irreversibility of everything, but also the certitude that wisdom is to flee changes, to not promise oneself tomorrows, to know that "we are only for ourselves". Existence has no other measure than itself; it will endure as much as a perishable body can endure. From the dust rising from the human agitation of pathways, Reis pits the silent portrait of two lovers seated face to face, tipsy from wine, their completely white silhouettes peacefully offered up to the gaze of the gods. The love with Lydia is a past life in the universe of shadows, in proximity with the world of the dead. A love which leaves an imprint upon the sensitive life of the calm of this verse from which it flows, knowing it and already no longer worrying about knowing it.

## A wisdom of the discreet life

The stake is to be able to hand back Nature its currency of indifference. In the company of each of these women, the poet applies himself to making, if not life, at least the soul of beasts. Two figures of happiness are possible, that of the animal and that of the sage.

A poem reunites them, brutally counter-positioned:

> Happy, lone is the animal [...]
> Anonymous to itself, and
> Entering into death like his house;
> Or the sage who, lost,
> In science, lays out his frivolous austere life
> Beyond ours as well as that of smoke
> Raising his frustrated arms quickly
> Towards a non-existent sky.

("So much sadness and bitterness...")

"Be a stoic without the harshness of stoicism" – the equation comes from Reis himself – it supposes becoming the most identical to the thing we know how to be. This wisdom is the science of the unassuming life. It is about "knowing how to pass in silence and without profound troubles", in "only ever looking for the nothing of pleasure or pain / In little characteristics, imbibing the instances of freshness". The essential maxim is the following:

> Content yourself with being the one
> Which you cannot not be.
>
> ("You will become there alone, the one
> you always had been…", OP, p. 142)

As soon as the dangerous, destructive thought has neared (that a man is merely a thing amongst things), it must be suspended. The proposition of the poet is to trace his pleasure in the smallest of things, to live slowly, almost without movement or noise. Man can work on becoming a silent pedestrian, enjoying life in secret. This discreet life is a non-search, a non-questioning, a non-thought.

The wisdom of Reis is a figure of conscious abdication, maturely deliberated, in which, as Caeiro asks him, all energy for thinking is used in order to not think.

> Sit down in the sun. Abdicate
> And be king of yourself.
>
> ("In your hands, retain nothing…")

Wise is the one who searches for nothing, because if he persists searching and thinking, "he will find ruin in each rose, / And doubt inside of himself". Going back to the heteronymy we could also say: under the master (Caeiro), he will discover the orthonym.

The knot which forms between the heteronyms is found here to be essential. It is by the loyalty to the "metaphysics without metaphysics" of the Keeper that Reis, in his manner, conceives of the non-search and non-thought as the single most profound and severe uses that mankind can make of itself.

## Poetic art

The paradox is that this apologist of non-thought is the defender of a poem entirely devoted to thought and formed directly around the idea. Is it not he who writes:

> When thought is mighty and sovereign
> Subdued the sentence searches for it
> And the slave rhythm serves it

> ("I impose on my proud mind...")

Contrary to Caeiro, who rejects the entirety of art for the poem because he wants to see it grow without calculation, Reis brings a considerable definition to the poetic art, as much in his work as in the polemics within which he engages the other heteronyms. The stake is not based on aesthetics, but ethics. He expresses himself as much on the formal negligence of the Keeper as he does on the open debate with Campos on the essence of the poetic.

Regarding *The Keeper of Sheep*, Reis affirms: "the objectivist must, above all else, render his poems objects, in giving them defined contours, having in view that they thus obey laws external to themselves." Another way to put it, the poet with the sunflower-gaze should strictly govern the aspects of the poem if not its form – a term that Reis does not use. Starting from here, a lively polemic is undertaken concerning the style in which thought acts in and on the poem, a polemic which has as its principal target the oeuvre of Campos. Contrary this latter argument, maintaining the idea "thought must be emotion", Reis advances, not without provocation: "With these lone ideas, containing only what is necessarily emotive in each idea, you will make poetry." He goes to great lengths to prove that even the musical element of the poem, its rhythm, emerges above all, from the idea:

A perfectly conceived idea *is rhythmic by itself.*

(Ricardo Reis' project of a preface
for Alberto Caeiro's poetic oeuvre[15])

On the other hand, he categorically refuses that rhythm may come from emotion, or be governed by it. This gives way at best to the "chant", which is to say, "a primitive form of poetry". According to Reis the poem could be the site of the staging of relations between thought and emotion: it directly proceeds from the idea. And the more the idea fuses with the language, the greater the poem. We have to go back to what the idea itself is in the work of Reis. They are little familiar gods which inhabit things, molded in a way to the thing, which first provides contours and definition to the emotion – the rhythm, the rhyme, or the strophe, merely being "the projection of this contour".

The reference of Reis' poems is the anacreontic ode (and not the Pindaric, reference of Campos): it authorizes a great variety of versification, of extremely different lengths, and the juxtaposition of short and long verse. The idea frees the poem from the bias of syntax that the romance language subtlety constrains on it. Here, as in the case of the work of Mallarmé, the idea articulates itself in an essential way to

---

[15] In Fernando Pessoa, Le Chemin du Serpent, trad. Fr. de Michel Chandeigne, Françoise Laye et Jean-François Viegas, Paris, Christian Bourgois, 1991, p. 191.

the syntax. From one language, another is sculpted: the Latin syntax "inhabits" the poem of Reis in the same way gods inhabit things. It is the agility and solidity of these constructions which exempts this poetry from being a pastiche of the Latin elegiacs.

## The clear and solemn mastery of the forms of objects

Reis never ceases to criticize with acuity the absence of formal rigor which reigns in the work of the Keeper: "He has not subjected expression to a discipline comparable to that in which he has almost always subjected emotion and the idea." He specifies: I know quite well this form has a singular rhythm, which does not confuse itself with rhythm of Whitman's free verse, nor with the rhythm of the free verse of the French Moderns." But this singularity is negative, it cannot be generally applied: "*This rhythm is born* [...] *out of an inability to place thought in stable molds.*" In truth, the oeuvre of the Keeper renders the assignation of the poem to the idea by Reis precarious: if he cannot attribute to him this flood of emotion regarding the idea that he criticizes Campos of doing, he can no longer make the man of the sunflower a poet of the Idea. Moreover, Caeiro's radical absence of concern regarding rime and verse makes him fear that an insidious confusion between verse and prose has established itself. Did Caeiro not declare: "I write the prose of my verse"?

The core of the debate is not metrics – Reis by no means proposes any particular conservation of a prosodic rule – but it should be clarified all this depends on whether or not there is or isn't a poem, that there is a poem and not prose.

Thanks to Caeiro, Reis sees himself constrained to recognize that the thought of the poem can strongly disrupt its form and that "stable molds" do not necessarily agree with him. Nonetheless, he maintains that the poems of the Keeper are, even to the point of their form, identical to things, or rather, "objects". Let us note in passing that to confuse things with objects, Reis has contempt for this thought: he portrays it as a superior objectivism, precisely where, on the contrary, it operates a dissolving of any figure of the object.

The demand for a greater "objective" discipline however finds no more precise a definition than the following metaphor: the poem must secrete its own formal rule, isolatable in itself,

> like the stone, once it falls, obeys gravity, which being part of the logic of its movement, nonetheless plays no part of its material personality taken in itself
>
> (Project from the preface of Ricardo Reis for the poetic oeuvre of Alberto Caeiro)

And yet, he is not sure that such a thing is the domain of the non-poetic art of Caeiro, when the latter states,

> I do not worry at all about rimes. In no case whatsoever There are two similar trees, one next to the other. I think and write like flowers have a color…
>
> (*The Keeper of Sheep*, poem 14)

If this conception and its becoming oeuvre do not satisfy Reis, we should conclude that he expected something quite different from the poetic form than what had been in question in his critique of Caeiro up until now. The poem in the work of Reis should be capable of nothing less than conjuring time and death. And yet, only the "concise attention to forms and to the attributes of objects" can offer the poet a "safe haven". The definitive character of the idea sealed within the line can transform the one who writes into an immortal being:

> On the firm column
> From the lines
> I do not fear the future innumerable influx
> Of Times and oblivion.

> ("Unwavering loner...")

For Reis, eternity is the fruit of an aesthetic: it proceeds from the "clear and solemn mastery of objects and forms". It is in order to gain this mastery that the poem must make itself an object, or even "the idea of the thing". Poems are like these trusting trivial offerings which the cadaver takes with it in order to pay the toll for crossing the river of the dead. The perfection of their form has the same value as the coin shoved in the hand of the dead: it guarantees the overcoming of darkness and ruin. Reis inherits from the poem of the Keeper as poem, which is to say as a form against death.

This poetry of the idea seems to be written in an incorruptible stone. While it shows sketches, repetitions, and variants of the mark of the chisel, suddenly, on one of the pillars upon which it etches, it inscribes eternity:

> Anonymous, the ode engraves a smile.

> ("Nothing, your hands implore nothing...")

## Maxims

It would however be completely false to represent this poetry as contemplative or votive. Almost constantly anguished, it is magnetized by this singular question:

> What can the scruple of thought do
> In the balance of life?

("Stills of azure, mountains in the distance...")

The poetry responds by rare maxims which list, against finitude, contingency, and death, several possible *acts*.

Maxim of mastery:

> Just be your own master.

("Just be...", PP, p. 294)

Reis sums up the act by which it is possible to appropriate for oneself the being of things and the universe. This is how he details the gesture:

> Without necessarily closing one's eyes
> Close firmly your hand
> In the mortise of your touch
> On the world which surrounds you
> Against your palm perceiving
> Another thing than your palm

("Just be...," PP, p. 294)

Maxim of equality:

> Reign or shut-up.

("Reign...")

Ambition is useless. The Caesar you are capable of being would be no other than the ordinary man that you are. In the same way that for Caeiro trees and the worker are equals, for Reis, in front of Being, everything is equal. Keeping to this equality is the lone superiority that might be attained.

Maxim of economy:

> Desire little: you will have everything.

("Desire little…")

To posses nothing and desire nothing makes us equals with the gods. The one who desires little possesses everything. But the one who desires nothing is free. To avoid desire is to avoid love as love of the other, knowing how to experience it only using one's self as measuring stick, and via a calmed relation to the contingency of things and the world.

Maxim of integrity:

> To be great, be whole: nothing
> In yourself, neither exaggerate, nor exclude

("To be great…")

The desire to rise up, by which humanity strives to render itself identical to the gods, determines the ensemble of ethical acts which Reis seeks to formulate. If this desire fails, why not give into the abjection of illusion and fear? Being everything in each thing, giving all of ourselves in the least of our acts, is for Reis an artistic maxim as much as an ethics. The beauty of the moon allows him to inscribe in the poem this double meaning of height:

In each lake the entire moon shines
Because high-up it lives.

("To be great...")

## Maxim of independence:

The desire of the other, however seductive,
    never
Accomplish it in your name.

("The desire of the other...")

In several other poems Reis experiments with the idea that it would be perhaps preferable to construct ourselves an arbitrary destiny, which would be held to the image of fate. But the act identified here, on the contrary, consists of being nobody's slave, not even to one's self. Every destiny being involuntary and intrinsic, we are limited to accomplishing it with uprightness. The maxim is centered on an imperative to which a brother of poetry, Pasolini, knew how to entirely consent: "Become one's own son."

## Maxim of supremacy:

Yes all that you do, do it supremely.

("Yes all that you do...")

Strangely, the maxim takes up the demand of integrity in order to apply it to memory and recollection. The challenge is remember a lot rather than a little. A more ample freedom of recollection assures the poet, "will make a lord of yourself". This act allows by the mastery of memory to reverse the stranglehold of time, in order thus to become no longer its slave, but its equal.

Maxim of indifference:

> Gaze at life from afar
> Never question it
> Nothing it can tell you.

("Follow your fate…")

At the heart of this last poem the idea that "we alone our equal to ourselves" is strongly present. This certainty resonates with the conviction that nothing external has made us and thus nothing external can unmake us. Instituting this equality of ourselves with ourselves is the act which allows us to escape from the inequality of the world and what we would desire it to be. Thus it becomes possible to show the same indifference towards Nature and the universe which they show toward us.

## I only want them to forget me

What renders death atrocious is that dead, "we die yet again", because death reintroduces man into a body whose existence he has forgotten. It is in front of the cadaver that the poet whimpers: "I clasped hands, not a soul, now they lie here in / earth." And yet, to do away with this obsessive fear of death comes by ceasing to fear the gods – which cannot be done without a long pensive confrontation with them, without a non-religious meditation of these fabulous fictions.

### The small familiar gods

In the work of Reis, all the gods are *cosa mentale*: they are what man constructs not out of his ignorance, but out of a sure knowledge of what man knows not to be. Reis does not credit the gods for overstepping human finitude, of palliating the non-sense of existence; he represents them rather as incarnating, of materializing a limit. And such is, in his eyes, their virtue. When men turn themselves towards the gods, it is themselves they see. The poet notes that, if prophets precede gods, no god, on the contrary, ever forecasts man, of which absolutely nothing in the universe can be the harbinger. Purely fictitious, the existence of gods in no manner refutes the total contingency of humanity.

More mental configurations than religious ones, the "gods" of Reis are foremost the being of each thing thought. They express what thought adds to things in thinking them, or even the mode in which thought heightens things in order to see them. The gods of antiquity have, in this respect, concerning the Christian god, the superiority of being numerous and thus have the ability of tuning themselves to the multiplicity characteristic of things and the universe. They are more likely to hold the idea according to which "a god is assigned to each thing that exists". These "tranquil and immediate gods" suit well the little familiar gods of the pagans without aura:

> Allow me the Reality of each instant
> And allow me my immediate and tranquil gods
> Which do not reside in the Uncertain
> But in the fields and rivers.

> ("You the believers in Marys and Christs...")

To restore life to these gods of antiquity allows the poet to imagine ideas in another manner than as abstract essences. Each thing mediates a little god, which is nothing other than the thought which thinks it. This god internal to the thing is not the "Idea" in the Platonic sense. According to

Reis, "erecting ideas in abstract persons", Plato merely follows "the old pagan process of the creation of the gods". The poet on the other hand strives to render the homogeneity of the thought and the thing, the interiority of thought to being meaningful:

> If a god is assigned to each thing which exists
> Why is there not a god which comes from me?
> Why would I not be god?
> In me, god comes to life
> Because I feel
> The exterior world. I see them clearly
> Things – men – without a soul.

("If to each thing which exists…")

Divine figures compose a strange list in this poetry: there is first of all the gods of the elements: Aeolus for the wind, Apollo for the sun, Neptune for the sea, and Jupiter for thunder; then all of the divinities from the kingdom of the Dead: Pluto, the daughters of Night, the Furies, as well as the character of Orpheus who challenges them; and then Saturn incarnating the devourer Time, and Pan who Reis refuses to believe is dead. Amongst all these divinities, it remains permissible to choose, as between multiple fictions, without anything making one privilege the most recent fiction amongst them, that of Christianity. Christ is nothing more than one more god, "one which was perhaps lacking". The preference of Reis nonetheless remains with the gods of antiquity, to the countless divinities of paganism, because these gods are more homogeneous than Christ to the idea of primitive chaos and the night, more conformed to the contingency of a universe in which "the gods (themselves) are nothing / But subordinate Stars of Fate." Reis shares with Caeiro the project of a "pagan reconstruction" around these figures, which have an ability, like the Keeper, to not think:

> Gods are gods
> Because they do not think.

("Follow your Fate...")

This paganism does not constitute a religious, social, or political project, following in the footsteps of Nietzsche. It has a purely metaphysical stake. When Reis declares himself "exiled" from what he calls "the ancient homeland of his belief" – which he identifies as the period of Epicurus – he reminds us that this philosopher had towards the other gods "an attitude of a god" that he showed himself capable of being:

> [...] serene and seeing life
> From the distance in which it is.

("Slightly golden is the pallor of the day...")

Following the example of the divinities they invent, man can always have the pride of seeing "always clear / Before no longer seeing". The gods are that in which man can equate himself if he accepts to conform their thought to the Being without meaning of things and the world. A poem sculpts this idea in words of marble:

> The greatest is the one who step by step progresses
> In the consciousness of the universe which is one's own
> And which push after push reaches
> The territory of the gods,
> Because the more he see things clearly
> The more the gods are condescending to him and make him a
>     peer

Until he feels his body
Brushing up against eternal bodies.

("The greatest is the one who..." OP, p. 184)

## Another humanity

Even poems which direct the gods and men mix up two metaphors whose meanings contradict each other: on one hand, that of the herd which lets itself be led, unaware of who leads it; on the other hand, that of the anthill which the foot destroys. In the same way that men without knowing it govern the life of cattle, it could also be supposed that reigning over us "and binding us / Other presences act upon us" of which we are unaware. But the ants whose shelter is destroyed take us for gods, which we are not, despite whatever the ants think. Like us, gods "Turn, suns, centers, slaves / Of an excessive movement". Inventions of men, gods are homogeneous to the being of the universe. Themselves contingent as well, they do not govern it.

Finally, this figure of the gods reproduces the human condition in accentuating all the traits:

From our resemblance with the gods
For our good, let us deduce
The thought that we are deities in exile.

("From our resemblance...")

This thought can change in our apparent destitution into strength:

Let us agree to believe
In complete freedom

> This present illusion
> Which equates us to the gods.

> ("Here Neaere…")

Far from being supreme powers, far from bearing a primary truth, the gods express the incapacity of man to reach truth:

> The gods give life, not truth
> And are themselves perhaps unaware of what truth is

> ("Under slight tutelage…")

Men are definitively neither more or nor less than the gods, and the gods are neither more nor less than men. In the work of Reis, it is men who make gods in their image, and not God who creates man in his. An imperfect shadow of a god, man has death as his proper imperfection. But what in the in the end distinguishes the gods is that they possess "the clear vain vision of the Universe" and know how to abandon it. In this quasi-Goethean conception of Reis', the gods are thus "another Humanity" by which humanity doubles itself from a fiction that expands it. This is why the poet calls them "just as real as the flowers but (only) visible for our highest gazes."

According to the way we live, these gods have contempt for us or, on the contrary, make it so that the flame of our life does not quiver. They help "their calm faithful", securing from their example "those / Whom have no other pretension / Than to get carried off in the river of things". And it is in taking them as a model that the poet renounces thinking, a decision which no longer adheres to ontological motives, as was the case for Caeiro, but ethical ones.

Not thinking is deduced in the work of Reis from the necessity to conform himself to the meaninglessness of existence. For him, life is a tributary of a larger river, which is death:

> Indecisive existence, fatal
> Tributary of the dark river.

Even the gods and their Messiahs pass away like the fictions they are and equally with them all the vain dreams "which are other Messiahs". At the end of the day, alone, "silent the earth endures". Thus there is nothing to think about but this nothing. *Reis shifts the thought of the Keeper without fleeing from it*:

> Tomorrow does not exist [...]
> I am merely the being which exists
> In this instant, which could be the last
> Of this man that I pretend to be.

> ("In this confused world...", OP, p. 169)

Against the powers that fear arouses on the edge of ruin, Reis affirms neither science nor the grandeur of the stars will triumph over them. Because science is "the sterile and distant contemplation of close things": it gazes at them but eternally remains incapable of seeing them, in the sense where the Keeper, himself, sees them. As for the stars, Reis makes fun of them for being "a vast vastness which tries to pass itself off as infinity (as if the bottomless could be seen itself!)": in a way, a false infinity.

Atheism, founded on science and the materiality of the universe, does not do away with the gods: it juxtaposes itself with belief without wearing it down. Reis does not deny the gods, he examines their appearances. He detects in these fictions the existence and horror of contingency. To succeed in brooding over these invented figures in order to escape from what it is so difficult for man to think, Reis steers him to the thought in front of which he agrees to stand up without flinching or trembling. He thus slowly erases the gods, making himself forget them at the same moment they forget him. This patient wearing down is the poetic task silently bestowed to Reis from Caeiro.

According to the assertion of the Keeper in which nothing is better than that which exists, Reis can thus add, from the interior of a severely acquired peace and freedom:

> Inert, I flow, without request, nor
> Gods towards which to address it.

> ("About the branch that she left...",OP, p. 150)

# 7

# The naked and real hour
# of perpetuated
# metaphysical emotion

## The poet as disciple

### Everything differs

Even by the admission of Campos, the utterance to which
Caeiro's tormented existence clings is the following:
"Everything differs and it is for this reason that everything
exists."

"Everything differs". In truth, this first axiom reunites two
theses of the Keeper: on one hand, each thing exists
according to its own limit; on the other hand, Nature is an
ensemble "without a whole". Like his master, Campos
brings a diverse proliferation to the poem, but he does not
strive to apprehend each thing in its singularity and in its
own limits. What he wants is to transcribe the multiplicity
of the multiple. He wants it to directly enter into the poem,
allowing us to feel it via of the poem. This effort is that of
the great odes, the oeuvre of his first years of existence,
which Campos also designates as his "supreme poems".

"[...] This is why everything exists". The poem of the Keeper does not differentiate being and existence; for him, "things simply exist". Thus existence fully belongs to Being. It does not add itself to Being as that which renders it possible. Existence in the work of Caeiro is not a possibility of Being, because a being without existence is not a being; a thing that does not exist is not. This thought ignores the possible as it denies cessation: existence is Being itself. In the work of Campos, however, this equation does not establish itself. Between being and existence, a rift opens up:

> If something has been one day, why is it no longer?
> To Be, is thus, not to be?

To be is linked with existing, not-existing, or capable of existing. Being is conditionally seated next to its existence or non-existence. From that which existence does not confuse with being, it follows that "the key to the gate of Being" remains, despite the oeuvre of the Keeper, still to be found. This importance of the relationship between Being and existence to Campos' poems gives them the deceptive outward appearance of existential poems, even though they always proceed from an abstract approach in which existence is merely a material amongst others. The introduction of a gap between being and existence exposes Campos to what he ends up designating as the figures of an "Ultra-transcendence" and an "Ultra-being".

The Ultra-being is a vertigo which forms within the interior of thought when it thinks existence as correlated to Being, and thus stumbles onto the mystery of Being as existing:

All existence is an abyss from the simple fact that it is able to be
From the simple fact there is being.

("Ah! In front of this reality…")

Ultra-transcendence is the temptation, up against this mystery, of summoning a Supreme Being who would render an account of Being at the point itself of existence:

There must be existence in order for the world to create itself,
And to exist is to be unconscious, because
It consists in rendering Being possible
And rendering Being possible exceeds all the gods.

("Ah! In front of this reality…")

The figure of the disciple strays from that of the master: what arouses only calm and contentment in the Keeper, troubles and anguishes the disciple.

## Stuffing consciousness with the universe

Caeiro works for thought to become a pure outside, devoid of any interiority, in such a way that it becomes identical to things and the universe. In the work of Campos, the aim of the poem is also to challenge any dualism between consciousness and object and to destroy thought as interiority. But the operation of the poem is the opposite of that of Caeiro: it is about "exploding" consciousness by stuffing it with the universe. The stunning, dizzying effort of Campos is to make enter into the poem "both everyone and every place". It is only in this way that he no longer feels indebted "to the frightening knowledge of seeing" transmitted by Caeiro. Every great poem strives to allow for the totality of things, events, and moments, to penetrate into the interiority of consciousness. Dilating consciousness with the help of a whirlwind of sensations until thought becomes entirely extraverted, extracted from itself, thought no longer discerns between its contours and what it thinks. The poem compensates via the intensity of sensations, via its science of "heating them up till they're red hot", the impossibility of it truly being both every place and everything at the same time.

Here subjectivity finds itself increased and at the same time dislocated, gutted, and dissolved. To increase the expanse and intensity of sensations jeopardizes the interiority, the closing in on oneself, of thought. But the poem stands up to the task of transcribing the infinity of the universe from the lone bias of a necessarily limited multiplicity of sensations, and this work reveals itself to be by essence without completion: "Something is always missing, a glass, a breeze, a sentence", admits "Passage of the hours".

## The essential disorganization
## of this poet

The poem fails in its project to contain all things, of being equivalent to the universe. Alternatively, what makes the poem beautiful is how it shows this attempt. The poem makes the operations of this reconciliation shine. It describes them as it accomplishes them. Nevertheless, after the great initial odes, the poet renounces this prodigious effort and settles for irony. Indeed his oeuvre experiences a sort of involution: it starts with very grand forms full of noise and fury, these "supreme poems" which are the "Odes", the "Triumphal", the "Maritime", or the "Martial", and ends in curling itself around poems which their author names "millimetric" and around some discouraged sonnets.

The poem, "Reluctance", when it expresses the ironic wish to "organize Álvaro de Campos", provides a very important indication about this heteronym: this poet is fundamentally "disorganized". And, paradoxically, it is the influence of the master on the disciple which is disorganizing. Campos is a poet whose field of thought is extremely distant from that of the Keeper, even when he accepts to expose his own poem to Caeiro's "metaphysics without metaphysics". The striking poem dedicated to Caeiro, "Master, my very dear master", thus analyzes this interior conflict: the Keeper woke Campos to a new consciousness that he had not possessed. He raised him above the "deluge of subjective intelligence". He made the thought of things and the gaze "the heart of (his) entire intellectual body". He thus transformed the "decadent and stupidly pretentious" poet that he was during the time of "Opium Eater" into a great poet. Campos had been "constrained" by the Caeiro-thought into being other than "himself". He nonetheless didn't become identical to Caeiro:

> "Oh, master, I would only be like you if I had been you."
>
> ("Master, my very dear master…")

The non-subjective poetry of the Keeper strongly works on the subjectivized poetry of Campos. But, in the heteronymy, each poet replays the part under his own name. The heteronymy proceeds by successive differentiations and boundaries. Campos is a new configuration of thought in regards to the questions of Being and metaphysics, thus he develops another poetic "situation", other operations, other figures of thought, and in the end, another manner of being a poet.

The confrontation with Caeiro is Campos' raw material – it transmits to him the gaze-thought and things, but it is also destructive – to the extent it engenders strong tensions between the ontology of the Keeper and a romantic configuration to which the poem of the disciple remains attached.

## Wrenching the poem away from romanticism

His entire oeuvre indeed bears the traces of a deep relation to romanticism that the title of the poem, "Reluctance", spells out so well in these terms:

> Romantic productions everyone of us!
> But if we weren't the productions of romanticism,
> Perhaps we would be nothing.

Master but not founder, the Keeper operates a rupture, which he does not entirely carry through. He remains isolated at the heart of the heteronymy itself. From the point of view of Reis and Campos, the poetic caesura instituted by Caeiro must be re-traced, re-identified, or even re-arranged. There exists a romantic site of the poem, from which the poem has not perhaps escaped. And perhaps from which, despite the innovations of Caeiro, it cannot abstract itself. The poetic gesture of Caeiro allows for an "everyone of us" of romanticism to survive. It is in regards to metaphysics that the inscription of Campos within romanticism enters into tension with the poem proposed by Caeiro. Campos, like his master, indeed displays an ironic suspicion regarding metaphysics: "Spare me the metaphysics" – the same for aesthetics, morality, science, art, and civilization – begs the grinding "Lisbon Revisited" written in 1923: "Let us be done with the metaphysics of sensations", demands "Barrow-on-Furness", a sinister palinode from the *"Maritime Ode"*.

Metaphysics is sardonically compared by the poet to the different possible mental effects of a malady with physical origins: a cold, for example, would be responsible for the idea that the mystery of the world exists and that the existence of the universe would be obscure. In metaphysics only the physics is taken seriously. Campos here seems close to the Keeper in estimating that only a disease could make the absurd question of purposes and causes appear to him. Conversely, the "metaphysical crisis" is likely to be cured by an aspirin or some baking soda. An image (present in an unforgettable fashion at the heart of "Tobacco Shop"), of a little girl eating chocolate, bears the cynical declaration that "there exists no other metaphysics in the world than chocolate".

Nevertheless, it is in the poems of the "second Campos" that this denial of metaphysics is active. These poems are beset with fatigue, with the desire to sleep, disillusion, disgust, the feeling of failure. They have explicitly abandoned the attempt that the great odes strived to deploy. In what we must call by contrast, "the first Campos", the tonality is quite different: each poem is an affirmation; each poem goes to battle, and this combat – whose complexity is extreme – is a combat for metaphysics. It is not one that is completely in favor of its pure and simple perpetuation, but in favor of what the poet calls metaphysical feelings or emotions.

## Metaphysics and "metaphysical emotion"

Metaphysics can be felt, this latter Campos maintains in a brilliant article from 1924 titled, *What is metaphysics?*, because the abstract and the absolute can not only be thought but felt. Such is the position of the *Odes*. Each ode in its own way produces this "metaphysical emotion". Several prose texts from Campos expose his proper project in these poems. The heteronym believes that the impasse of metaphysics is relative and temporary. It is in part an effect of the period, which he characterizes as dominated by religious feeling. Campos reunites under this name a "religiosity of the Beyond", the onto-theological belief in a primary and Supreme Being, and what he designates as a "religiosity of a future humanity", which, in his eyes, expresses itself in utopian political thought. This religious sentiment goes hand in hand with an emotion he analyzes as being produced by "the Abstract as non-concrete", which he also calls the "Indefinite". To the extent that it has romanticism as its starting point, the poetry, like the time period, is inhabited by a taste for the abstract as non-concrete. This diffuse religiosity devastates and ruins the properly metaphysical figure, including the one found in the poem.

Campos' diagnosis is that within this current sequence, "the material of metaphysics is not completely defined, nor in a state of being thought". Nonetheless, the poem can produce emotion. Against the domination of religious sentiment, against the emotion coming from the "Indefinite", the task of the poem will be to construct a feeling of the "Abstract as abstract", an emotion of the "Defined", which would assert metaphysics if not as a thought, at least as a feeling.

So it is that the "Maritime Ode" begins regarding the Indefinite:

> Alone, on the deserted dock, on this summer morning
> I look out along of the sandbar, I gaze towards the Indefinitude,

and advance until the "real and naked hour" of unheard of metaphysical emotion, within the disrupted silence which encloses it. It is of course not a coincidence if the poem opens with the romantic posture, par excellence: that of the poet standing, solitary, turned towards the sea, gazing and dreaming. The grandeur of the trajectory is to construct bit by bit, in distancing itself from the initial site of the poem, what Campos calls, "the abstract Distance", it alone capable of freeing thought from the deceptively abstract influence of the religious.

## Does a Platonism of Campos exist?

For Campos, the poetry of the Keeper presents itself as a wonderful "attention given to the always multiple exterior world". Is this definition valid for him? It seems Campos sees himself rather as:

> In the daily sorrow of the mathematics of being,
> Slave to everything like a dust from all the winds.

> ("Master, my very dear master...")

This name of the "mathematics of being" around which Campos has recourse in order to characterize his own work is remarkable. We will compare it to the grouping he formulates between metaphysics and mathematics: "Mathematics at its highest level, confines metaphysics", he writes, "because what metaphysics looks for is precisely abstract formulas". Campos' poetic attempt is not to give birth *in loco* to metaphysics, to "abstract formulas of Being", but to create "Abstract moments" from it. These moments, entirely constructed by the poem, are those in which an emotion of the Definite is capable of being produced. Campos thus strives to establish a sort of bridge between a destroyed metaphysics and an as yet unknown or impossible future metaphysics. If Caeiro presents himself as the Keeper of a "metaphysics without metaphysics", Campos is for his part, a kind of Watchman:

> Continue...You said
> That in the development of metaphysics
> From Kant to Hegel
> Something was lost
> I am in complete agreement.
>
> > ("I would like to love to love...")

The heteronym in this poem states that beginning with Kant up until and including Hegel, metaphysics has suffered a loss. Kant introduces a dualism that, splitting Being in two, declares it outside the reach of thought. The critique of Reason destroys metaphysics far beyond its explicit intentions in spreading a skepticism: not so much by a radical limitation of what in the real can be thought, but by the dissolving of this equality of being and thought which rendered the ontology possible.

The great figure ruined by Kant on this point is Plato. And yet it is towards him that the disciple of the Keeper turns himself. The poem titled "Two excerpts from odes" evokes this with nostalgia:

> The hour when Plato has seen in a dream the idea of God
> Sculpting a body, a clearly plausible existence
> At the heart of his thought external to him like a field.

Revisiting *Platonism* as a poet, Campos inscribes the intelligible in the sensible, weakening their opposition: the Idea "sculpts" a body; thought exists as equal to a field; the "Grand Dock" of the *"Maritime Ode"* is also a real dock. The hour magnificently depicted crystallizes a metaphysical capacity towards which the poet melancholically turns round and round, with the dull regret that his own thought cannot be related in the same terms to Being and the universe. Campos does not know how to traverse this "Platonic hour" of the poem. When it appears in front of him, he admits being ignorant of "which sensations to have or to pretend to have". His desire would sometimes be to let himself be seduced by this state of metaphysical thought,

> Whose shadows come from something else than things,
> Whose passage does not brush up with the trains of their
>     gowns the ground of the Sensitive Life
> And leaves no scent whatsoever on the paths of the Gaze.

("Two excerpts from odes")

## Places which are in a way
## outside time and space

In many different ways, the poems of this heteronym conserve as an internal reminiscence what it is possible to call the "Platonic moment" of metaphysical emotion. This takes the form of an involuntary and quasi-unconscious symbolic carrier of quite ancient metaphysical meaning "which troubles in me", Campos says, "the one I was".

Night, for example, whose gown is "laced from the Infinite", bears all the seductions of the One. It

> Lays the distant mountains at the feet of near trees,
> Confounds within a field [...] all the fields which I see,
> Erasing all the disparities of distance that I perceive.

Thus creating

> An inexact and confusingly disturbing expanse
> Within an expanse which is suddenly impossible to cover

> ("Two excerpts from odes")

The Platonic figure thus manifests itself as a kind of "spontaneous" metaphysics of the poem. Campos seems to think that it is consubstantial to it, or more precisely, consubstantial to that within it which is an impulse toward ecstasy. Against the Keeper, he maintains that once a poem encounters mystery and meaning, it does not return to an obscurity or opacity of Being but, on the contrary, attests to the possibility of passage between existence and essence, between existence and being:

> Ah! In the hours colored with silence and anguish
> What essential mystery and meaning coagulated
> In a divine revealing ecstasy
> Is it not a bridge between any dock and THE Dock!

affirms the "Maritime Ode".

The places which organize these poems of Campos are conceived by him as located "outside time and space". The same can be said for the enormous, industrial, agitated city within which the Platonic "Great Dock" of the "Maritime Ode" resides as well:

> The Absolute Dock the model from which unconsciously imitated,
> imperceptibly evoked,
> We other men have constructed
> Our own docks of actual stone on real water,
> Which, once they are built, suddenly appear
> Real-Things, Mind-Things, Entities of Stone-Souls.

The same can also be said for the strange restaurant where one serves the poet cold tripes in style of Porto. These places are deliberately shielded from the two "*a priori* conditions of sensitivity" defined in the work of Kant. Caeiro declares: "I do not need time in my plan." Campos rejects both time and space: the Moment of metaphysical emotion constructs an integrally "abstract" site.

While in the work of Caeiro "philosophy" and "metaphysics" are generic names which do not refer back to any proper name and elicit an overall critique, in the work of Campos references to Plato, as well as Kant, Hegel, Epicurus or Aristotle are explicit. But to invoke Plato beyond and against Kant does not mean that the metaphysical emotion, which the poem has the responsibility of constructing, can be produced by the mere evocation of this figure. The Abstract Moment around which the poem works and orients itself is not the "Platonic hour". The disciple of the Keeper notes the ontological rupture imposed by the gaze-thought. He is much too "modern" to inscribe himself within a pure and simple continuity of *Platonism*: in addition to being tormented by the question of the infinite, he is, like his master, freed from the figure of the One, attentive to the multiple.

The solution invented by Campos in the "Maritime Ode" is to reconstruct and retrace the Platonic site in order to let it be uprooted in opening the poem up to the "intoxication of Difference", the infinite proliferation of the multiple.

### Knowing where to be
### in order to be everywhere

Beyond the seductions of the Platonic hour, Campos' poem in effect records the existence of "our moments of root-feeling", which appear when

> [...] in the outer world, as though a door had opened
> And, without anything changing,
> Everything becomes diverse.

The apprehension of the multiple character of Being is at the origin of metaphysical anxiety. The same anxiety can appear "as nausea but in spirit", when thought expects starting from a position of vision predicated on a distance and gap, for example like that which is created between a departing boat and the dock, from the possibility of a gulf between Being as unity and Being as multiplicity.

In order to respond to this anxiety and to the challenge of diversity, Campos' poem strives to be equivalent to the universe, to its untotalizable and inexhaustible multiplicity. Thus, ideally, it must be a "complete synthesis made from an analysis of the whole Universe without any omission", hence the heteronym writes semi-seriously, semi-ironically. But this multiplicity of the universe presents itself without links: between things and in things there is only the void;

the poem finds itself doomed to a diabolical scattering. As the "Martial Ode" radically utters, the universe is "an innumerable river without water – only people, things / Terrifyingly without water".

In the end, "things" in Campos' work are not "natural": "Nature" has been completely abandoned for Caeiro. The things of the disciple come from the universe of big cities and from mechanization. Their essential characteristic is precisely not being "what they are", but in excess of what they are. Grasped in their multiplicity and no longer in their singularity and limit, apprehended in their proliferation and no longer in their own self-identity, things appear as being "excessive". This imposes on the poet to not only know "how to feel everything in all manners", but to "feel everything excessively", as expressed by the poem titled, "All things considered, the best way to travel is to feel".

The poem proposes a figure of exhaustion equal to the multiplicity of things and the universe. It must produce this multiplicity not as a succession, but as the simultaneity of existences. And it must attest in doing this that it is not its own consciousness that it encounters, but indeed the external alterity of people, things, and the universe.

The *operation of exhaustion* passes by the cataloguing and indexing of the real: it is about rendering perceptible an abstract equivalent of the "multicolored and anonymous river" of the universe. The sites of this cataloguing can be the crossing of a large modern city, of its cosmopolitan and colorful crowd ("Ode of Triumph"); the fascinating variety of maritime travels, whether it be from other times or today ("Maritime Ode"); the abstract trajectory of speed, of a fantastic overlap of pure energy, throughout the universe ("Salutation to Walt Whitman ").

The *operation of simultaneity* is announced and named as such in the poem:

> To be the same thing from all possible ways at the same time,
> To realize in oneself the humanity of all instants
> In a loan diffused, prodigious, complete, and distant instant

("Passing of hours")

Or still:

> I want to leave with you, I want to leave with you,
> At the same time with all of you
> In all the places where you have gone!

( "Maritime Ode ")

Then, there are types of transformations and equations which carry it out:

> I turn in the helixes of each boat.

("Ode of Triumph")

> I am mechanical heat and electricity.

("Ode of Triumph")

> Now, at the brief height of the dream of your actions,
> I am losing everything of myself, I no longer belong to you,
>     I am you,
> My femininity accompanies you, being your souls themselves!

( "Maritime Ode ")

## Being practically
## an act of abstract orgy

The operation of grasping alterity passes by the elicitation of a masochism, whose core is the recurrent wish in the work of this poet, of wanting "that one should maddeningly make [him] belong to someone else".

The "Ode of Triumph" thus summons "masochism via the bias of mechanisms", articulated to the "sadism of some modern *je ne sais quoi*". The poem details the desire and pleasure of imagining oneself being ground by the gears of a motor. This masochistic figure, more intellectual than sexual, inscribes how it is for the poem to "physically penetrate" itself with all that is external to it, to rip itself up, to entirely open (itself) to becoming permeable" to things and the universe. These impulsive machineries are metaphorical of the poem and the poet: "Being as complete as a machine", "In order to completely express myself as a motor".

The central movement of "Maritime Ode" deploys a gigantic abstract orgy in which the poet first becomes (figure of exhaustion) "the woman-all-women" / Who were raped, assassinated, wounded, ripped apart by pirates!" At the same time, he is also (figure of simultaneity) "the pirate-character at the height of piracy, / And the victim-synthesis, but in the flesh and blood of all the pirates of the world!". The poet explicitly labels himself as an "an absurd Christ of expiation of all crimes and violence":

My cross, I carry it in me, wounding, burning, cutting,
And everything hurts me in my soul vast as the Universe.

("Maritime Ode ")

The masochistic metaphor resonates within another utterance by Campos: "To gaze is for me a sexual perversion". The gaze is the initiation of a violent movement by which things, people, and the world are going to penetrate the poem with force. A movement which gives to the poet the joy of feeling himself become, as he says regarding Whitman, the "spirited concubine of the dispersed universe", or even: the "grand pederast rubbing (himself) against the adversity of things, / Sexualized by stones, trees, people, jobs", the "incubus of all gestures", the "whore of all solar systems...". The poet represents himself with delight as the "pimp" of the universe.

"Salutation to Walt Whitman" exposes the profound intellectual aim of these operations:

> [...] I do not want any interval whatsoever in this world!
> I want penetrated and material contiguity of objects
> I want physical bodies to be one to the other like souls.

The poem must show that "all Matter is Spirit", and more still, that Matter and Spirit are nothing more than "muddled names".

## The abstract Moment (1)

In order to be equal to a universe which presents itself as "a vast supreme ground [...] neither high nor low / But under the stars and suns, under souls and bodies", the poem must transform itself into "a formidable dynamic restrained by an equilibrium", a "non-distinct summit, saturated with the infinite".

This moment in which the poem is able to destroy consciousness in making it explode under the weight of the universe is the first abstract Moment. To produce such a moment requires that the poet have an "oblique mastery of our intellectual senses". This obliqueness is the mark of what is needed to abstractly match the real at the same time this abstraction must be constantly tested as tangible. "It must "concretely be an act of abstract orgy". The poem "leaps with everything above everything", thus becoming for itself an entire universe. Such a leap exists in the "Ode of Triumph", in "Salutation to Walt Whitman" and, albeit in a more complex manner, it is present in the interior of the "Maritime Ode".

What's more, the poem immediately judges its success or failure. Either it is able to proclaim ("Ode of Triumph") that this first abstract Moment has been reached:

> The Moment of a naked and burning torso like that of a
>     blacksmith,
> The dynamic Moment,
> Where I no longer know if I exist turned toward the exterior,

And it can in this case cry out with jubilation:

> [...] Hooray for me once and for all!

Either it can ("Salutation to Walt Whitman") announce its confidence in the possibility of reaching it:

> My path spreads to infinity and up until the end!
> Whether I am capable or not of reaching the end, this is not
>     your business

> With me, with God, with the ego-senses of the word Infinite...
> Forward!
> [...] Abstract apogee at the end of me and everything.

Or it is the source ("Maritime Ode") of punctuating the complete dissolve of any distinction between consciousness and the world:

> The entire world no longer exists for my eyes. I am burning
>    up.
> [...]It is with such an excessive and frightening speed,
> That the machine feverous from my overwhelming visions
> Presently turns, that my conscious-wheel
> Is nothing more than a circle of fog whistling in the air.

Or, on the contrary, it records a failure: consciousness has not been dislocated by the intensity of sensations; the poem did not know how to produce plausible equivalents of the diversity of and infinity of the universe. Or perhaps fatigue carried him away: "I have felt too much to keep feeling".

Campos' poems inscribe the question of their success or failure within their development. The tense, precarious, critical character is a singular trait of this heteronym.

## The naked and real hour

Despite appearances, the abstraction of Campos is not exactly its use of raw ordinary existence, but its already "poeticized" substance in poetic configurations that he uses secondly as an already used material. Thus, the great modern city, factories, motors, the crowd presented in "Ode of Triumph" come from the futurists. The sea, sailors, voyages – all things "naval" from the "Maritime Ode" have their source in British Romanticism of the *Rime of the Ancient Mariner* by Coleridge, in Stevenson's pirates. As for the plebian promiscuity of "Salutation to Walt Whitman", it comes from Whitman himself. It would however be deceptive to reduce this to system to borrowed goods.

## Sites and saturations

Coming from the futurists, the British romantics, and Whitman, Campos continues the investigation all the way to the cross streets and exhaustion of three possible sites of the poem. It is this movement which will be noted here under the name of saturation.

The "Ode of Triumph" takes the trip of futurism and its protocols. Campos multiplies the equations in the cookie-cutter style of the futurists. However, the greatness and beauty of the ode resides in the distance that is gained from then on vis-à-vis futurism whose inventions were ingenious but whose thought was quite thin. The same Campos will then make fun of the becoming-academic of Marinetti in a poem ("Marinetti, academic"), which takes up one of their favorite procedures, onomatopoeia.

"Salutation to Walt Whitman" is an extraordinary self-portrait: of Campos as Whitman, much more than Whitman himself. The evocation of this "brother in front of the Universe", of the "great epidermic democrat, contiguous to everything", of his "ferocious and tender fraternity with everything", allows the heteronym to describe of what his own poem is made. Indeed, it is Campos, not Whitman, who aims at being both

> The subject and the object, the active and the passive,
> The it and the here,

Circle which closes all possibilities to feel
The mile-marker of all things which can be
God term of all objects which can be imagined [...]

The gigantic crowds, the laborious wandering underground humanity of Whitman, all this "marvelous fauna from the depths of the ocean of life", serves as material for Campos when he strives to penetrate the universe within the feverish consciousness of the poem. By doing this, Campos projects a strange metaphysical grandeur onto the American poet.

As for the romantic poets, the question is more complex. The extraordinarily subjective, albeit abstract, character of Campos' poetry indeed connects him with the romantics. His is a poetry which in its own way supports this descent of the infinite in the finite so characteristic of romanticism. We remember that he was the heteronym with which Sá-Carneiro felt the utmost profound affinities. After the suicide of the latter, it is possible that the oeuvre of Campos develops as a sort of Tomb of the young man. The "Maritime Ode" thus includes a long crossing of the romantic site, the poem, applying weight to it in order to rip itself away from the primary Platonic moment. The ode thus transforms into a kind of sweeping conscious romantic poem before achieving, under the effects of a new courage, the "naked and real hour" of the dock without boats.

### The dock, the wheel, the crane

A poem about a poem showing both how the site of the thought of the poem is constituted and how the poem works: the singular greatness of the "Maritime Ode" can be found in the fact this heteronym deploys itself here in its maximum complexity. The "Maritime Ode" organizes itself into four movements whose intellectual articulations are possible to locate but also may be perceived in their different tonalities as from the interior of a vast musical composition. Immediately following the overture, a first movement resuscitates the Platonic moment of metaphysical emotion. The second movement appears in the form of a romantic poem dedicated to capturing multiplicity and diversity. From the interior of this site, a second moment of metaphysical emotion is constructed, freed from the melancholy which surrounded the Platonic evocation, but not from every figure of Transcendence. The poem then liberates itself from romanticism in order to turn towards what it names "the European hours", era of progress and machines, which it ironically scrutinizes for its metaphysical capacity or incapacity. Throughout the traversing of this indecisive contemporaneousness, the poem cogitates the three sites that it has just traversed and turns itself towards its own duty: to inscribe within the "naked and real hour" the abstract Moment of metaphysical emotion which no longer adheres to the figures of thought of the past, but maintains a hypothesis of a future metaphysics.

Opening the poem, there is first of all the arrival of a boat entering from a distance into the port, barely visible, and whose abstraction is being as "non concrete" for the gaze as the Indefinite image it incarnates. If the poem opens itself as such to the romantic posture par excellence, it is due to a very specific word. Armand Guibert's translation, which replaces "infinite" for "Indefinite", is a true misinterpretation. But it is a misinterpretation full of meaning, putting the finishing touches on the romantic posture instead of making it stumble. However, in the language of Campos, the Indefinite is not synonymous with the Infinite: it is the opposite of the Defined, of this "Abstract as abstract" around which the poem must steer itself. When the "Maritime Ode" begins, the poet, turned towards the Indefinite, keeps himself at a maximum distance from the emotion of the Defined, which the poem has the responsibility of liberating.

The dock where the poet lingers quickly becomes a site of metaphysical anxiety which is not merely elicited by the imperfect vision of the boat, but all the arrivals and departures of ships. The gap that their distancing digs between ships and dock becomes for the mind the obscure symbol or unconscious revelation of a gap between the existence of things and their being. This gap finds itself for a time reduced by the apparition of the "Great Dock" that infiltrates each dock with the Platonic Idea of the Dock. A figure "outside of time and space", each real dock seizes the possibility of being essence and being, existence and idea. For the poem, the Idea itself, which is to say, the "Absolute Dock", is in truth just as real as things: the "Great Dock" exists amongst the other docks; it is also made of "actual stone on real water". The "real" docks and the Idea-Dock are inseparably "Real-Things, Spirit-Things, Entities of Stone-Souls". This evocation stamps out anxiety until the moment where Platonic construction gives way to the pressures of the multiple that swells in this poem invaded by voyages and boats.

Thus, the ship that approaches is transformed into "all the boats of all navigations" and the people on board are transformed into sailors of all periods, of all genres, warriors and merchants, discoverers and pirates, world travelers and explorers. These mutations little by little fill the poem with a fever and drunkenness before the infinity of a world that constantly and violently multiplies itself. So begins the properly romantic sequence of the poem during which the dual figure of consciousness performs its devastation, its "red explosion" under the mass of sensations and intensities of desire. Once this new abstract moment has been achieved, the poem experiences a sudden relapse. The time of childhood causes an eruption: a happy and revolved period of metaphysical emotion which is in some ways innocent and anterior to all anxiety. In the poems of Campos, these melancholic visits to childhood create a kind of pause: a respite for thought. Nevertheless, it would be "somehow a metaphysical impression than substituting childhood for the desire to understand the world". The poem turns towards childhood as towards its peaceful origins. It appeases itself. But its courage is to turn away from its childhood.

### The abstract Moment (2)

After this interruption, the impossibility of restarting the dissolving machinery of the poem, except in a "literary manner", is revealed. The anxiety of the mystery thus takes the upper hand and infiltrates the poem, restoring the threat of Transcendence. The romantic site reveals itself to be exposed, unlike the Platonic site, to the eruption of figures of a Supreme Being and a first cause.

Faced with this risk, the poem once again shatters its own path. It separates itself from the ship in which it came and from the stream of violent reveries in order to turn itself towards the maritime life and the contemporary world. The spontaneous production of the period is a vaguely cosmopolitan humanitarianism combined with a religiosity. The life aboard grand transatlantic ships becomes the symbol of this. That the core of metaphysics remains in certain cases untouched and unchanged, however, is what the lines of "Maritime Ode" express, reminding us that "the old sea" and that "the Distant is always in the same place / – Nowhere, thanks to God!". From this it concludes "poetry has lost nothing, what's more it has even gained machines…". Modernity constitutes, in regards to metaphysics, an undecidable time.

All that remains then is to follow the path suggested by the vision of the new ship, the "so humble and natural" English steamer preparing itself to leave the estuary. Like it, the poem simply needs to accomplish its duty, which is to inscribe within the sky "the semi-circle of an unknown emotion" which returns to the solitary poet to perpetuate. The abstract moment here is achieved in the plenitude of its abstraction, and is the reason why the hour can be said to be "naked and real": freed from the nostalgia of the Platonic hour, plucked free from the false romantic infinity, conceding nothing to the a-metaphysical humanitarianism of modernity.

Two internal "machineries" of the poem, the wheel and the crane, serve its successive poetic operations. The movement of a "wheel", (the helm is taken amongst other naval things by which Campos draws forth the dominant materials of the ode) sings a dozen renewals of the changing rhythms and intensities of the poem. It is nothing other than poetic consciousness itself, the self-consciousness of the poem. The acceleration of its rotation underlines the progress accomplished in the destruction of the dualism of consciousness and the world. The wheel then slows down its movement considerably when the poem penetrates to the heart of "modern maritime life". It completely immobilizes itself when it takes leave from the era in order to decide its duty in solitude.

From the wheel comes the pendulum of the crane with which the poet writes his last words directly on the sky. But the entire poem will have been a "crane-poem", a poem capable of transporting thought above Platonic and romantic configurations to make it execute, without resignation, a veritable "semi-circle", confiding from then on in the metaphysical emotion which his "compass" knew how to plot.

Different from the other great odes, the singularity of the "Maritime Ode" is not to reduce the abstract Moment of metaphysical emotion to the Platonic hour nor to the dissolution of the pair consciousness/universe. This poem has the power of arranging an ultimate Abstract Moment in which the desire of metaphysics affirms itself without this desire remaining a prisoner to nostalgic or regressive figures. There exists thus at least one poem capable of carrying in a non-reactive manner the will that a new metaphysics exists beyond the ruins of metaphysics. This is what is of a decisive importance in the "Maritime Ode".

### Equations and symbols

Everywhere else, a certain hesitation remains for Campos between the idea that metaphysics must and can be perpetuated, and the idea that it should simply and purely be ridiculed, abolished, and denied. This uncertainty comes from having less clarity in his work than Caeiro concerning the distinction between metaphysics and philosophy, and the devolution of ontology to the poem. The possible terms of a demarcation between philosophy and metaphysics are not completely pronounced, thus the poem rids itself of philosophy with much difficulty. Its weakness is in never establishing an ontology that belongs only to it. But this is also where we find its grandeur: it presents and traverses the main metaphysical configurations, no longer polemically like the Keeper does, but in order to underline and show depressingly, their expiration.

The hesitation of the poem between symbol and equation materializes this division. The recourse to certain symbolic images translates a certain homogeneity of the poem to Platonism. These images exhibit an ingenious Platonic substance of the poem by way of its split between the identity (to) itself of Being and its essence or between things and their existence. Campos affirms:

> Symbols, everything is symbols...
>
> ("Psychetype (or psychotype)")

Just as soon to cry:

> Symbols?
> I have had enough of symbols. […]
> Symbols? I refuse symbols.

("Symbols?...")

On the contrary, the equations render possible the different operations of simultaneity, exhaustion, and grasping of alterity which are necessary for the novel production of metaphysical emotion. They reveal, during the course of the poem, terms that the poem assimilates and, even something much rarer, how it assimilates them. They definitively justify the name "mathematics of being" under which Campos enigmatically labels his own oeuvre.

## The poem as debris

To equate the poem to the entire universe: this desire introduces a clause of infinity. Because the task is endless, going up against the proliferation of things, the impossible totalization of a multiple universe, up against its "painful instability".

To be incomplete, Campos maintains, is in any case, "not being God". The infinite he gauges is an infinity without any meaning and, in this manner, homogeneous to the "things" of Caeiro-thought. It juxtaposes itself to the universe; it does not express it and it is not an empirical trait of it. Because the poem is incomplete, beset by an unachievable task, it is at least homogeneous with the infinity that it gauges, which is itself neither natural nor divine:

Let's go! May the ride have no end, not even in God!

("Passage of hours")

Campos attempts implementing a non-theological figure of infinity:

Let's go, advance!
Even if God himself prevents us from it, it is of no importance,
Let us go on
Let us go, straight ahead! And nowhere else!
Infinity, Universe! Goal without goal! What does it matter?

("Salutation to Walt Whitman")

As a consequence we have an artificial infinity, which is to say, one which is necessarily constructed. We should analyze whether the Definite would perhaps actually be the figure of the infinite in the work of Campos, in its opposition to an Indefinite which he prefers in this case to write as "in-Definite". Is it perhaps that the "Definite" is the infinite as the poem is capable of writing it?

## Ah! to not be the only one who is everyone and everywhere at the same time!

But Campos is not sure that his poem is capable of proposing a non-transcendental figure of the infinite. And perhaps it is only mathematics and not the poem that is capable of this. In *Salutation to Walt Whitman*, the center of the "splendid and infinite cogwheel" that the body of the poet has become thus finds itself situated "within some sort of spatial dimension from a God-of another manner".

Where does the enthusiasm shatter which inspired him a thousand times, directing him "towards the Abstract, towards the Unobtainable", toward "the invisible Goal – all the points where I am not"? Why does the poet make himself dependent on the desire to "resolve the equation of this prolix anxiety": being himself at the same time all things and places?

It is "discouraged poems" which abandon the terrain of the multiple and the infinite and let themselves be invaded by the regressive feeling that existence would be the expression of a hidden mystery in or under things. We see – as in "Lisbon Revisited", or in the poem that bears, under the guise of the title, this precious annotation: "Clearly non-Campos!" – that poems dare claim via great screams this "Indefinite" which elsewhere Campos fights as a plague of the mind:

> I have an avid and carnal hunger
> Of what I do not know
> Defined by the Indefinite.

> ("Lisbon Revisited", 1926)

> (I feel) a desire of the Indefinite
> A lucid desire of the Indefinite.

> ("Clearly non-Campos")

Here we find a kind of intellectual riot forms itself against the hypothesis itself of the "Defined":

> When we have well defined everything, we have not yet defined
> What explains why this is everything,
> Why there is something...

> ("Ah! In front of this reality...")

It is a brutal return to the transcendental question, which the influence of the Keeper keeps at a distance. From the interior of the oeuvre of the disciple, these poems manifest the desire of totalization that is sometimes stronger than acceptance of the inconsistency of the multiple:

> What a shame all things are merely fragments,

deplores one of them ("The flourishing of the fortuitous encounter..."), regretting to have only captured "the interstices, approximations, and functions of chance and the absurd". The entire universe becomes once again just as opaque as if it were "the inner night" of a jail cell. Being transforms into a prison, as well as the desire to reflect upon it. A poem like "Barrow-on-Furness" attests much more to a floundering of thought than to its discouragement. It is, to once again use an expression from the "Tobacco Shop", "a broken gateway to the impossible"

Sleep, fatigue, inertia, a renunciation of thought gains ground: "A great fatigue, of being so many things." If the heteronymous poem gives way to the will of totalization, it no longer records anything more than "the sum of all disillusions, [the] synthesis of all despairs". All that remains for it, another poem bitterly states, is to strive to "make children to Practical Reason with the energy of those who believe in god".

### The force of the millimetric

The poems of the "second Campos" do not all give way to this regressive figure. The poems Campos calls "millimetric" resist erosion and discouragement. This adjective does not indirectly state a reduction of the ambition of the poems, but another level of the same thought. "Millimetric" is, in the second Campos, what persists in refusing transcendental poetry, most of the time using humor. They are always attempts to escape from romanticism, but, we could say that this time, it is via the low brow, in ridiculing it.

"Tobacco Shop", in this way, is a decisive poem. Is it a poem about renunciation? From then on, one must reject any *existential* reading of this poem. The "I" of the poem, here as in all of the heteronymous poetry, is the "I" of the poet. Consequently, the "I am nothing", "I will never be anything" in which the poem begins should be understood as utterances concerning the poet as poet.

The evaluation of the figure of the poet comes to grips with the regime of nothing, in the same way the oeuvre will be in a good number of Campos' other poems, assigned the status of "debris". The poet is nothing because he is nothing other than his poem. This neither flows from a posture nor a decision: "I cannot *want* to be nothing." The poet is first of all nothing because he is one of "of the millions of beings in the world of whom no one knows who he is". The essential anonymity of the poet – to contain in himself "all the dreams of the world" – does not distinguish him from the dreaming humanity which is sheltered by "these garrets and non-garrets of the world" or from "the geniuses–for–themselves" who are also in the middle of meditating or writing. The "windows of the room" of the poet give way to the real, but to a disappeared real. They have their sights set:

> On the street inaccessible to the mind,
> Real, impossibly real, obvious, unthinkably obvious

The window frames a meeting between thought and the world of sensations, the poem and the real, in which thought is perplexed, paralyzed, and separated from things. The poet describes himself as a splinter between:

> The loyalty that I owe
> To the tobacco shop in front of me, as a thing which is externally real

and the pure interiority of his thought:

> The sensation that everything is a dream, as an internally real thing.

There is no other "fraternity" between him and things than a "farewell". The street, this street seen from a window, reveals that a "mystery of things" resides under stones and beings, including the mystery of destiny and death. This gap between thought and the world imposes a malaise in which all positive perception of the oeuvre and the life of the poet devours itself: "I failed in everything." Following a long drift of this negative figure, the trust in the possibility of thinking the real reconstructs itself. Such is the general line of the poem.

Was the way the poet proceeded correct, to withdraw himself from all learned things, from any field of knowledge or education? Was he correct in "exiting through the back door of the house"? Could the disinterest of the poet lose itself in a figure of nothingness?

> Since I have had no ambition whatsoever, perhaps everything has been nothing.

In order to put an end to the paralysis which keeps it separate from the real, does the poem have recourse to turn itself, in order to question it, towards thought itself? Would one opening be to confide only in thought? But nothing assures that thought can be a thought of Being and of the real. It is no use convoking the category of "Genius", the inspiration of the Muses, or the sublime – all categories through which the poem successively passes in reexamining them not without parody and mockery.

> I am not sure if the Muses truly appeared.

another poem comically meditates ("The Ancients invoked the Muses"),

> [...] But I know that we do not appear.
> How many times, leaning over the wells
> Which I suppose myself to be,
> I have bleated: "Ah" in order to hear an echo.
> And I heard nothing more than what I saw:
> This faint dark gleam which made the water shimmer, there, in
>     the uselessness of the depths...

The same irony is freed up in "Tobacco Shop":

> As those who invoke the spirits invoke the spirits,
> I invoke
> Myself and find nothing!

Perhaps it is better to return to the window, which had been abandoned as a place of a too demanding faceoff of thought with the real. Returning to the visible, the poet persists in feeling a frightening impression of foreignness: I "see the street with an absolute clarity" and, nonetheless, "all of this is foreign to me". Maybe there exists, as the poem affirms from the beginning, a derisory disproportion between the effort of man to think the universe and the eternally mysterious character of this same universe. We are merely the "cardiac slaves of the stars":

> We have conquered the entire world before getting out of bed;
> But we wake up and here it is opaque,
> We get up, and it is alien.

The temptation to renounce all thinking of Being and the real traverses the entire poem at the same time the character of "the little girl with chocolates" appears in the middle of the street. It is to the child that the poem addresses this cynical commentary:

> You will see that there is hardly any other metaphysics in the world than chocolates.

Continuing, the poet finishes by finding, via the critique of the sublime, a supporting point for thinking his own thought. The sublime here is nothing else than art giving meaning to a world devoid of meaning:

> And I am going to write this story in order to prove that I am sublime...

To which we find the opposing idea that the lines in the poem are already there, already "found" by the poet, "as a thing ready-made". They are anterior to his thought, outside his will, and thus, certainly "useless" in their "musical essence", but in no way meditated or "sublime". And yet, without the gift of such lines, the poem would stumble miserably in the paralyzed faceoff of thought and the world. All that remains then is to elucidate where this gift comes from. The poem indicates that only an imperceptible modification in the real itself can rearrange the real for thought:

On other planets in other systems [...]
Always one faces the other,
Always one just as useless as the other
Always the impossible just as stupid as the real,
Always the mystery of the depth just as obvious as
    the mystery sleeping in the surface.

But then something else emerges, which was not "in the painting" and which changes its initial givens:

[...] a man entered into the tobacco shop.

This minuscule detail emerging from the sensible with its opacity, its enigmatic allure, will be kept by the poem. It is the way in which the real this time clearly addresses a gesture to thought. The man who enters the tobacco shop enters the poem at the same moment – changing the impossible real into a "plausible reality" which "immediately falls" on the poet. Liberated, from then on he can get up from his paralytic chair and return with confidence to the window, where this time he will receive the salutation of the obscure "Esteves-without-metaphysics", who, "as if guided by divine instinct", succeeds in making a gift to the poet of the real. A smile finds its way to the face of the Tobacco shop owner like the Smile of the Cat in *Alice in Wonderland*, a smile which is that of the poet himself in front of the universe *in extremis* reconstructed as thinkable by the poem.

"Tobacco Shop" thus does not conclude with doubt or renunciation, but with the affirmation of the eminent ability of the poem. This ability is not at the level of the ideal or hope; it is confidence in the resources that the poem possesses, crossing in an instant of its journey its own "Esteves-without-metaphysics".

## A universe trying to pass through

Campos is battered by his own thought; he expresses all kinds of suffering, including the anxieties of failure and despair of not finishing. His poem sometimes slips through his hands – like the image of cup slipping through the hands of a server and whose shattered pieces the gods contemplate with a distracted curiosity at the foot of the stairs. In the end, his oeuvre, in his eyes, takes on the figure of debris or trash:

> My oeuvre? My primordial soul? My life?
> Trash.

> ("Annotation")

However, neither complaint nor bitterness prevails over this tormented poet's will of "passing". That we are dealing with an excessively subjectivized poetry should not make us forget this trait that Campos underlines:

> I have always seen the world independently from myself.
> [...] never has my suffering made me see in black what was
>     orange.
> First and foremost, the external world!

> ("Despite everything...", *PAC*, p. 258)

"First and foremost, the external world": this indeed the motto. To fully render justice to this poet demands that the accent be placed on his desire before the apparently impossible task which he is assigned: to inscribe word for word a non-transcendental infinity within the poem.

Unifying in an underground manner the impulse of the great odes and the density of his millimetric art, Campos is loyal to this magnificent declaration:

Open all doors to me!
I will finish by passing through them
[...] I am Me, a thinking universe in flesh and blood, wanting
to pass through.

("Salutation to Walt Whitman")

# 8

# Portugal
## as a possible site of truth

In 1934, Pessoa, taking the risk of a misunderstanding concerning the main orientation and meaning of his oeuvre, published[16] the lone book to appear during his lifetime: *Message*, a national poem. He presents his book as a sort of public rivalry with Salazarist nationalism at the poetry competition organized the same year by the Secretary of National Propaganda from the Salazar government. The volume earns the "prize from the second category"– this prize is given to compensate works which are under 100 pages, and this category was created by a friend of Pessoa in order for his work to figure among the laureates of the competition.

The circulation of his book seemed more urgent to the poet, or more opportune, than the organization and appearance of *Fictions of the Interlude*, whose impending completion he had announced to Gaspar Simões. In January 1935, during a letter exchange with Casais Monteiro, who was curious and questioned him regarding this choice, Pessoa

---

[16] This was the only *book* (but not the only poems!) Fernando Pessoa published in his life.

acknowledged *Message* was not the best introduction to the ensemble of his oeuvre: "I am in fact", he clarifies in a letter from January 13, "a mystical nationalist, a rational Sebastianist. But I am, outside of and in contradiction with this, still many other things," to which this book, in its proper substance, provides no idea whatsoever. *Message* is nonetheless the first book he succeeds in composing and completing with an eye towards publication in Portugal. The explanation the poet provides for this is the following, and it is important: the book "coincided, without me planning or premeditating, some critical moments (in the original sense of the word) of the remodeling of the national subconscious."

The decision to publish *Message* had thus been rendered possible by an element which was extrinsic, in appearance: a crisis situation affecting what Pessoa labeled as the "national subconscious". The poem, this specific poem, revealed itself as adequate to this situation, already prepared for it, without which it would not have been able to "coincide" with it. Furthermore, this coincidence appears to Pessoa of such import that he takes the risk of publically exposing his book in circumstances (the competition) favorable to a misunderstanding by the political and intellectual apparatus of Salazarism.

Ten months later, Pessoa announces to Casais Monteiro, after a speech by Salazar on censorship and the *Estado Novo*, his formal decision to no longer publishing anything, and, no doubt, to no longer write as well. This voluntary withdrawal at the age of 43 closely precedes his death.

## Poem and politics

Pessoa maintains a very intense relationship his entire life with the question of Portugal as a nation. The withdrawal of the country, its provincial isolation, was a painful reality for him which he swore to fight. His decision began from very early on with his return to Lisbon after, a long exile as child in South Africa. He is barely 20 in 1908 when he notes in his Journal: "My intense patriotic feeling, my desire to improve the situation in Portugal, have arisen in me – how does one describe such warmth, such intensity, such sincerity...? - a thousand plans. [...] Outside of my patriotic projects – to write *Portuguese Republic* – [I would like] to provoke here a revolution, writing pamphlets in Portuguese, editing old national literary works, creating a magazine, a scientific review, etc." This is not an exaltation of a young man, but the first formulations of a program for an entire life. The same year, the students at the University of Lisbon go on strike against the dictatorship of João Franco. This strike, in which Pessoa find himself as one of the leaders, will fail, leading to his departure from the university. This little known political incident was the source of Pessoa's decision (whose studies where all done in English) to write from then on principally in Portuguese. Armando Côrtes–Rodrigues recounts, in *Notes presented to Joel Serrão*, how Pessoa "had first thought to write only English poems" and how "it was the Franco dictatorship (of João Franco) which threw him into literary patriotism; he then began to ardently desire to write in Portuguese, which didn't take place until September 1908."

Soon after, the society "Portuguese Renaissance" was established in Porto (in 1912) as well as the review *A Águia*, both carriers of the program to "provide [by literary means] a renovating and fertile content to the republican revolution". Pessoa was enthusiastic for the project and published several articles of literary criticism in the review, whose impact was immediate. A text titled "The new Portuguese poetry considered sociologically", was a work in which Pessoa deduced the inevitable appearance of a great poet – a poet greater than Camoens, a "supra-Camoens"–, which would excite the academic authorities with rage, who would declare him presumptuous and megalomaniacal. No one had as yet known of a poem by Pessoa, and his description of Portuguese society and politics was ferocious. According to this article, the poetic movements marked by the *saudade* were due to a "period of impoverished and depressed social life, a period of cheap politics, and where obstacles of all sorts opposed themselves to any sort of daily peace (whether it be individual or social) and to even a rudimentary confidence, any certainty as to the future, or even to a future as such."

In the next installment of this polemic, Pessoa will be driven to specify his proper criteria for evaluating Portuguese politics in terms which are important to cite here because they will not vary much throughout his entire life: "To be a monarchist in Portugal today is to be a traitor to the national soul and to the future of the Portuguese country. [...] The republicanism which will be the glory of our land and by which new elements of civilization will be created is not the current, corrupted, idiotic, and denationalized republicanism which is that of the tri-party republican. It is necessary to understand this point well: if being a monarchist is to be a traitor to the national soul, a co-religionary of Mr. Afonso Costa, Mr. Brito Camacho, or Mr. António José de Almeida as well as the horrendous underling trade unionists, socialists and others, represents a parallel treason, equivalent to the first. *Their spirit is absolutely at the antipodes of the new literary current. Everything about them is imported from abroad and without elevation or grandeur.* [...] The republicans are in no way anti-traditional; they meticulously resumed the old methods of despotism, corruption, and crime that the monarchy preferred so much as its methods." Pessoa concludes with call to "remain completely Portuguese and rigorously republican, and an uncompromising enemy to the current republicanism ("Relapse..." in *A Águia*, 1912). His diagnosis will not have changed much when he edits his "Biographical notice" in March 1935, several months before his death: "I feel," he then writes, "that the monarchical system would be most proper for an organically imperial nation as Portugal. At the same time, I think that monarchy is absolutely not viable in Portugal to the extent that if we organized a referendum about the regime, I would vote albeit with sorrow, for the Republic."

Thus, in Pessoa's eyes, the national question is a decisive indicator of the different policies. To him, all appear to be weak or faulty in this matter; the future of the question for him can be found closely tied to the emergence of a new Portuguese literature.

## *Art and the national*

The gap which Pessoa felt between an innovative literary current, very much attached for its part to the national figure, and the policies presumed to incarnate the revolution and the Republic will soon be completely patent: the publication, under his and Sá-Carneiro's responsibility, of the journal, *Orpheus*, attracts the almost unanimous attention of the "moths"– a nice name by which the two friends label the old-fashioned Lisboan academic opinion – and incites a scandal in the nation's capital. The tension is aggravated even more by the onset of war between France and Germany: faced with all of Europe being engulfed in this sinister conflict, this generation of young artists, poets, and intellectuals demand responsibility from the bourgeoisie. One of the first strikes from the heteronym, Álvaro de Campos, is to give to the journal, *Portugal futurista*, a pamphlet titled *Ultimatum* – which represents one of the most virulent manifestos ever to have been written against the war. This text challenges the idea that whomever would fight in this conflict would be for freedom or duty. It violently attacks all those he judges responsible for this war, whether politicians, generals, writers, or philosophers. So it is that he lays out a kind of catalogue of the "mandarins of Europe", demanding "their immediate expulsion" due to their criminal incompetence. Amongst them, of course, are heads of States and war, the Joffres and the Hindenburgs, but also the intellectuals who rallied to the conflict – Anatole France, Maurice Barrès, Bourget, Kipling, Shaw, Yeats, d'Annunzio, Maeterlinck, Rostand, Loti – without forgetting philosophers of the highest order such as Bergson, in the sad company of Boutroux and Euckens.

This charge against war does not save a Portugal characterized as "loose-change Portugal, remains of a Monarchy rotting into a Republic, sordid last rites of a wretched artificial collaboration in the war but with its natural shames residing in Africa". Faced with the stagnating condition of this country, the poet fights his disgust to rebellion:

> I am choking having nothing but this around me!
> Let me breathe!
> Open all the windows!
> Open more windows than exist in the world!

(Ultimatum)

As a reaction to the political exacerbation of nationalisms, the review affirms wanting to create a "cosmopolitan art": "cosmopolitan in time and space". Only the diversity of currents can serve as a support to a revitalization of thought.

## Europe and the universal

*Ultimatum* declares the "general collapse of everything due to everyone" and, symmetrically, "the general collapse of everyone due to everything"; in brief, "the total collapse of peoples and destinies". It is not, however, a nihilistic pamphlet. The moment of this collapse is analyzed as a sign announcing that Europe is perhaps striving to overcome its limits and to finally become something beyond "its geographical label [...] to be a civilized person." A question emerges which *Message* will attempt to answer 20 years later: what today could indeed be the equivalent to discovering a "New World"? "Who from now on still knows how to inhabit a Sagres [the cape from which the first Explorers departed]?" asks *Ultimatum*. The "program" around which it concludes, as it takes up parodying the Nietzschean category of the Übermensch in a half-buffoon, half-serious manner, provides, as content, the heteronymy: in the intellectual desert created by the general consent of war, is not the issue then that each poet is capable of being several poets at a time?

### The separation of politics and the poem

Beginning with Campos' *Ultimatum*, the faltering of Portugal is analyzed as arising from the renunciation of any figure of universality. The recurrent inability of Portuguese politicians regarding Portuguese policies was scrutinized: in particular, the "revolution" of Sidónio Pais; then the seven years (1926-1933) of the military dictatorship preceding Salazarism. This analysis is not done within the interior of literature or poetry: we are dealing with texts of political or "sociological" analysis – to use the names under which their author labels them – in which Pessoa forges his own categories of thought about these Portuguese political situations. He continued this work in parallel with his oeuvre as poet throughout his entire life. This separate co-existence of poetry and politics comes from a political thinking separate from the exercise of the poem. The fact that Pessoa had the project of thinking politics, but located what the poem thinks outside the field of politics, certainly makes him a unique figure amongst the poets.

Each heteronymous oeuvre practices a separation of politics and the poem not so much by an indifference concerning the political, but by the grand intuition that a new political thinking could not exist without constituting a completely different thought, forging its own categories in the analysis of political situations. This desire towards a separation is explicit in Caeiro's work, where poetic egalitarianism challenges political egalitarianism in poems which stage the faceoff of *The Keeper of Sheep* with the "man arrived from the city", also called "the preacher of truths". The Keeper provocatively accepts injustice "like he accepts a stone is not round". He wishes to possess the "natural egoism of the flowers / And the rivers which follow their path / Preoccupied only without even knowing it / Of budding and flowing". The singular "mission" that he conceives is to exist and to know how to exist without thinking about his existence, thus conforming himself as much as possible to the being of the world and things. This concentration regarding a thought of Being which would not be "thinking" is the mode in which this poet put an end to metaphysical distraction. Politics, however, in his eyes, like metaphysics, participates in a questioning in terms of cause and effect, of object and subject, of consciousness and the real, against which the "metaphysics without metaphysics" of the Keeper absolutely rebels.

In the work of Reis, poetry shies away from politics under the guise of stoic indifference of the world: a striking portrait of this indifference is provided in a poem which exalts two chess players, cut off from the world in the course of the game, who ignore the torments and the destructions caused by the war that rages around them.

In the work of the orthonym, the subtraction of the poem from politics has nothing singular about it; the poem, conceived as the vain public register of the furtive traces of the existence of the non-existent, is external to any politics as it is with anything.

While Campos intervened scandalously on several occasions into Portuguese politics, his poetry ridicules politics conceived as philanthropy which the "Russian novelists" – "one Dostoevsky or one Gorky" – are in his eyes the paragons. This poet posts, following the example of Baudelaire, a mocking repugnance, a light-hearted refusal of any pity or charity in front of the figures of the poor or homeless.

The entire heteronymy thus proclaims that the categories of fraternity and equality which belong to it, in no way correspond to how these categories are used in politics. So it is that Caeiro states that the sun alone is capable of justice because it shines equally on all things and people. And Campos, in the "Maritime Ode", states "fraternity is no longer a revolutionary idea": it is a type of ontological trait of being.

This non-confusion of politics and the poem in the work of Pessoa is accompanied by a desire and capacity for political intervention, proof of which is provided on several occasions. Besides *Ultimatum*, Campos wrote and courageously distributed in his own name a tract in defense of a poet against whom the students of Lisbon fought after he publicly declared his homosexuality. Under Salazar, Pessoa edited in solitude an extremely argumentative protest against the interdiction by the government of the Freemasons.

Does the publication of *Message* show for the first time the temptation of the poetic oeuvre itself for political engagement? What, in the eyes of Pessoa, authorizes the public staging of this work is the possibility of it participating in the "remodeling of the national subconscious". What can "remodeling" signify here? Salazarism works on the national figure by its own means and ends. The poem intervenes in this same situation by its own means and ends. Politics and poem thus simultaneously intervene around the figure of the national, without politics or poem in any way being identified one to the other. There is a particular moment in the question of the national, which runs through both the political and the poem, summoning them to intervene.

If Pessoa hopes to constitute on the basis of *Message* a completely different subjectivity counter to the national figure that Salazarism imposes, the mechanisms of the Pessoan figure are nevertheless apolitical. This is why Pessoa, next to the word nationalist, places the adjective "mystic" in regards to himself. *Message* contains a proposition concerning the national, which is first of all a desire of a universalist intellectuality, tied to several singularities of Portuguese history. Reflecting on the essence of the past greatness of the country, this poem strives to define the contemporary terms of the capacity of Portugal for the universal, the condition for a renewal of national existence meriting this name. Its proposition is at the antipodes with the nationalism in which Salazar is ready to plunge Portugal for many long years. But it is also equally foreign to any politics and to any contemporary political process of its formulation.

## Poem and myth

What *Message* utters regarding the national does not let itself be easily grasped. The linking of several figures of Portuguese history demands one to uncover and understand around what principle the comparison is organized. *Message* is indeed arranged as a sort of "cipher" of Portugal. This book can only be read via a deciphering by which, upon completion, the essence of the national will either be found or irremediably lacking.

## The reasons for the esoteric organization of Message

Regarding the existence of this coding, the transformation, *in extremis*, of the title of this book is significant. At the last moment Pessoa changed the title of his book from *Portugal* to *Message* – arguing that the oeuvre may not be up to the standards of the name of the homeland. But the genesis of the name *message* (*mensagem* in Portuguese) allows for another, more profound reason to be noticed: *mensagem* is derived from the Latin *mens agitat molem*, which means "mind moves matter". Such is Pessoa's conviction regarding the possible relationship between his poem and Portugal: if the poem has any chance of transforming the national subconscious, it is because the Portuguese nation, in each of its great periods of flourishing, had been modeled after an audacious mind, by a powerful intellectual project which governed it. This vision of Portuguese history presides over the character choices placed in the foreground of *Message*, as it does by those left aside. *Message* contains within it what is needed to motivate Portugal. But this is only the case if a "hidden Portugal" can be uncovered within it by a careful reading. The address of *Message* is subterranean and subversive. This coding allows Pessoa to secretly put into place the denial of everything that Salazarism considers to be a manifest representation of the national. The composition and organization of the poem aim to disrupt, not adopt the figures of the national arranged by the political nationalism.

The poems from *Message* were written during a period of 20 years, the first in 1913, the last in 1934, and a great number at the end of 1928. The poem concerning the return of King Sebastian, which indicates the call which concludes the book :

> O Portugal, today you are a fog…
> The Hour has come!

is already formulated by the poet in 1928. This very broad emergence over time of the poems precludes any relation with the crisis felt by Pessoa in 1934 concerning the national Portuguese subjectivity. It is after a long meditation, well before the existence of Salazarism, that at the end of 1934 the poet initiates his own appeal concerning Portugal.

*Message* showcases the history of the country from its most far-off origins, but it does not do it under the guise of the epic. It isolates and emphasizes a small handful of events, of which the poems strive to define and present the essence.

Moreover, the composition of the book not being chronological, the ensemble dismantles any orientation of the history, any idea of a progression leading to current time, of a culmination of Portugal in its contemporary state.

Its first part – "Blazon" – presents, according to the poet, the main intellectual resources of the Portuguese nation, a disposition which is itself spatial and which is that of the four parts of the Armory.

The second part – "Portuguese Sea"– strives to grasp what is unique about the Portuguese Discoveries, what in them differentiates intellectual discovery from imperial conquest. This is essential: it is this alone that determines the conjunction of the national and the universal as positive trait of Portugal.

The last part – "The hidden King" – reviews the different "announcements" or prophecies concerning King Sebastian, in order to define for the current times the possible rational idea of a "return of the hidden King".

### The myth of the fifth Empire

The book introduces an allegory about Portugal: the first "field" from Blazon contains the image of a Europe spread out gently in the form of a Sphinx, leaning in the direction of the West. The face or, more precisely, the gaze of this Europe is none other than Portugal. This representation illustrates the double character of the European site, traversed by a tension between its actuality, which is romantic, and its Greek origin: "a romantic curl covers [its] Greek eyes." A tension inscribed, as we know, within the heteronymy by the contradictory existences of Campos, "produced from romanticism like everyone of us", and of Caeiro, an improbable Parmenidean attempt. Italy and England upon which the Sphinx leans are historical figures of a universalism of which the British and Roman empires anticipated.

In order to completely grasp the image of the poem, one must try to represent what Pessoa tried to work out via the theme of the "Five Empires", from which the Sebastianist myth is inseparable. According to a prophecy which has distant biblical origins, a fifth Empire should succeed those of Greece, Rome, Christianity, and England (also designated as the empire of Modernity). The Portuguese legend makes it coincide with the arrival of King Sebastian. This new Empire would be capable of dissolving the other four, which were still only approximate figures of the universal, with all that remained external and foreign to them, thus constituting the "first truly universal and global empire". This hypothesis is that of a "universalization of European civilization", of a capacity for it to manage a universal deployment which would finally succeed the empires of conquest.

## A "rational Sebastianism"

"I feel", wrote Pessoa to Sampaio Bruno as early as 1914, "that a mysterious and perhaps important national phenomenon named Sebastianism is pulling at me." In 1934, *Message* proposes to transform the myth of the return of the disappeared king into a real capacity to "conquer a Distance" from within the disorientation affecting contemporary Portugal.

The myth arises with the death of King Don Sebastian whose reign was from 1557-1578 and who saw the first difficulties of the country in India, the extension of its plantation in Brazil, and the initial stages of a project to penetrate Africa. A strange character, a dreamer who fled women and society, Don Sebastian represented his country as the leader and savior of Christianity threatened by Arabia. Beginning in 1572, he strives to gather an army from all over Europe to go "fight the heretics" on the African terrain. A first expedition fails in Morocco in 1574. At the age of 24 years-old, the king recruits an enormous army of 17,000 men, but he fails to convince Phillip II of Spain to engage in this second attempt in Africa. In 1578, his army, commanded without any common sense, is defeated within a span of a couple of hours, during what we can barely call the "battle" of Ksar-El Kebir. It is a dazzling annihilation. The king is killed during battle, and his body disappears without a trace and is never recovered. He leaves no successor whatsoever in his wake. Immediately, the debate of whether or not Portugal should remain independent or join Spain becomes a burning question. The almost quasi-totality of the noblemen and women hope to rally behind the King of Spain. The people alone favor independence.

This situation is conducive to the diffusion of a "prophecy" formulated several years before the disaster by a shoemaker, named Bandarra, from the village of Trancoso. His prophecies, titled *Trovas*, announced the coming of the Desired One (O Desejado) and the imminent establishment of the fifth Empire – the shoemaker thus interpreted the prophecy of Daniel interpreting a dream from

Nebuchadnezzar. Within a national situation rendered precarious by the death of the King, noise begins to circulate that the Desired One was none other than this Don Sebastian who had just mysteriously disappeared, and that he would reappear in order to guide his people "numa manha de nevoiero"– through morning fog. In *Message*, the first of the *Notices* recalls this prophecy and the memory of its "scattered and anonymous" author, "whose heart was not Portuguese, but Portugal" itself.

In the following century, Bandarra's book, despite being banned, was commented upon and re-edited by a great erudite, the priest António Vieira, who took up a study of the *Trovas*. This Father Vieira, who wrote in a splendid prose, also led Pessoa to believe he recognized a genius of the Portuguese language. So it is that the second Notice is titled, *António Vieira*, and describes "the immense space of meditation" of the one who was "the emperor of the Portuguese language". Pessoa had assembled a quantity of notes with the aim of writing a book under the title of *Major commentary on the prophecies of Bandarra*, and he also edited several fragments for a text about the fifth Empire. The third Notice, which announces that the hour has come for the fifth Empire, is none other than his own.

In the 19<sup>th</sup> century, during the French invasions, the theme of the fifth Empire resurfaced, one more time linked with national sentiments. The myth traveled all the way to Brazil where it appeared during a popular revolt in the Northeast. Later, the magnificent film by Oliveira, *No, or the vain glory of command*, meditates on the hidden king, following very closely the historical figure evoked in *Message* – even though Pessoa is presented as a mere *technician* in the credits of the film…Which indicates the magnitude and persistence of the "national phenomenon" which had attracted the poet beginning in 1914.

Pessoa decides to invest in this myth which circulates around Portugal as an active belief. How should one use it and for what ends? Using the Sebastianist myth, he constructs the following entanglement: "Don Sebastian is Portugal: Portugal lost its greatness with the loss of Don Sebastian and will only regain it with his symbolic return." And what will allow for this return is the universalist vocation of Portugal attested by the essence of the Portuguese Discoveries: Pessoa maintains that "The Discoveries are a cultural act […]. *"So it is that we have created the modern world; because our first discovery was to discover the idea of discovery."*

Portugal, from then on an obscure and forgotten country, may perhaps hold the resource which alleviates the sterility of a West devoid of a future and which becomes again the "past of the future". Yet there remain three conditions for this to happen: Europe must establish itself as a universal figure, which is still uncertain; the Greek eyes once found in the Portuguese face must come back to life, which demands determining (as the heteronymy itself strives towards) what it would be like to overcome romanticism; Portugal must also decide that its future is in front of it and not within a rehashing of some lost grandeur, and this demands identifying without error the new figure of its destiny. At the root of *Message*, the meditative uncertainty of the Sphinx presents itself as an opening concerning this possibility: the reconnection of Portugal with its universal ambition.

## Myth and inception

In *Message*, myth does not do away with the recollection of a lost identity; it does not propose a return to an imaginary origin. An attentive reading of the poem, *Ulysses*, is essential in this respect. The figure of Ulysses as a mythic creator of Lisbon guides the meditation which also bears on the idea in *Message* of a possible foundation of a new destiny for Portugal. The poem shows the being of myth is not about possessing an independent existence, but being capable of fertilizing the real, even if it is in itself nothing. Through the fable of Ulysses creating the city of Lisbon, the myth lays out a double non-existence: the non-existence of Ulysses who is a hero of a fiction and the absence of the arrival in this place of a purely fictional being. And yet, as the poem underlines, this non-existence functions:

> Without existing it is enough.
> In not coming, it nonetheless came.
> And created us.

If it is the void within it which acts upon it, the power of the myth is a retro-active power. So it is that only a reality fertilized in this manner certifies the myth. This "nothing" which is more powerful than life, which itself being "only half-nothing will die in passing away". Because the myth verifies *mens agitat molem*, it proves the mind gives life to matter. This is the reason why Pessoa could ardently desire to be a "creator of myths". The fable of the creation myth of Lisbon by Ulysses constructs an entirely fictitious link between Greece and Portugal, but this imaginary link is what allows it to be retro-actively rendered as real, according to a chain which goes from Pessoa to Greece, passing by Ulysses, Lisbon, and "Person".[17] Ulysses prefigures the role which the myth of Don Sebastian is susceptible to play. This legend of a king whose foolhardy disappearance haunts Portuguese history could perhaps be at the origin of a new national figure, if the poem clarifies what this destiny could and should be.

Thus the myth for Pessoa is contrary to a primitive utterance of identity; it carries with it the possibility of a beginning. This is why the poem, "Ulysses", splits it up into two parts, one part inert, which he names "legend", and the other part, active. The "legend" is a retroactively unearthed yarn within the real, provided this real is revealed of being able to make its own determination. Thus it is always a "dead body", while the myth in itself is identical to the body of a "living and naked" god. It is not about repeating the myth, but splitting it in two: its active part will find itself put into movement once it is clear to what extent the myth indicates what could have taken place; its inert part – the legend – once used in this manner will thus return to nothingness. The myth is not some underground prescription of an origin or identity; it is a material with which the poem can think the possibility of a renewal that requires nothing.

The evocation, from Viriatus to Dona Philippa de Lencastre, of the heroes of crisis from which Portugal established itself, deepens the figure of beginnings. The

---

[17] In Portuguese, the word "Pessoa" can be translated as "Person" or even "Persona".

central idea which is affirmed throughout these poems is that "all beginnings are involuntary", that the beginning always exceeds the conscience of the ones who begin.

## The national, the universal, the poem

There exists something completely mysterious in the emergence and the real of a nation for the reason that "it is only in the self, that each person is the entire world". This also indicates that each nation expresses an aspiration which exceeds the concept of the national. Here we are dealing with the idea that each nation is equivalent to the entire world. The national would not be the confinement of the self, but, on the contrary, an overcoming of its narrowness. This paradoxical identity is neither communitarian nor substantial; it expresses or locally bears the world if not in its entirety at least in its generality. In regards to Portugal, this self-overcoming internal to the nation can be read within the necessity that "the world again looks for" a "new ocean which remains to be discovered". The Pessoan figure of the national props itself up via a singular vision of what the Portuguese Discoveries had been and from their possibility of providing a possible ulterior destiny.

## The essence of the Discoveries

Three worrisome silhouettes of the heads of empire, motionless in their gigantic statuesque postures, dominate *Message*: that of the Infant Henri, the "lone Emperor [...] / Who holds in his hand the world globe"; that of Jean II, who looks from beyond the sea and whose "formidable solitary mass / Fills from his present being the sea and sky"; and that of Alphonse d'Albuquerque, this king of such power that he wants everything / he can", to whom Chance "snares three earthly Empires", which he then contents himself in edifying, "as if out of contempt". These three apparitions express the imperial material power dominating a submissive world. But do they manifest, via the Discoveries, some sort of consciousness providing an opening for a new era of humanity?

"Portuguese sea" determines the question: it is stated that since the Infant under whose reign "one sees the entire earth, / Emerging, completely round, from the deep blue" all the way to the last vessel in which the King Don Sebastian boards in order to disappear, the Portuguese Discoveries will not have as their object the terrestrial empire of conquest. It is the spirit and audacity of science which hurled the navigators into the sea. Their boats departed not for material power, but the quest for truth. It was not about conquering, but knowing. If Bartolomeu Dias, the captain who overcame the terror of the Cape of Good Hope, can be compared to Atlas, it is because he was capable of "lifting and bearing the world on his shoulders".

Pessoa pits what he describes as a prodigious intellectual adventure against a quasi-initiatory quest, the voyages of those he ironically names, in a poem written under the title, "These Columbuses". In regards to them, he denies the ambition of the spirit, presenting them with a bit of disdain as those who "will finish by having / What we should lose". The weakening of Portugal and the reduction or collapse of its earthly empire are not the essential events, since this as well was not the desired goal. Rather, it is of the essence of what these Discoveries were that what follows them is transitory and that the material empire can belong to others. What matters is having "discovered the idea of Discovery", the figure of innovative intellectuality which expressed itself here. It is from this figure or idea that one should inspire oneself anew. "The finite sea is Roman or Greek". On the other hand, *Message* affirms the characteristic of the "Portuguese sea" to be "in-finite", because it is the ocean of an intellectual quest where knowledge and universality are at stake.

Imperial Portugal undoes itself. Nevertheless, the meaning of the first Discoveries is the destiny of this country to "accomplish itself again", which is to say, finding new paths in which one can look forward to "deserved kisses of Truth".

### Gesture and Time

*Message* strives to reconstruct the original subjectivity that lead to this adventure of Discoveries. Was it an isolated and improbable act? Once the time came, was it merely, as the poet says with humour, "the time that it was"? Or, was it, on the contrary, a figure of destiny, constrained by external undecipherable factors? Pessoa strives to recapture the gesture upon which this event depended – which the poem, "Occident", calls the untanglement: "We untangled", he writes. Should one be lead to think that Science inspired this gesture and that Audacity guided the hand which dared to project this light on the unknown? Or, should we believe that God was the soul of this enterprise and Portugal was merely the body? A hand raises the "trembling and divine" torch towards the heavens while the other brushes aside the veil of ignorance: the poem, in taking the position of tapping into the undecidability of the gesture itself, retains the confidence of rolling the dice again, of re-playing the turn.

### The poet and the national

Five characters, all kings or infants of Portugal, are, within *Message*, self-portraits of the poet: alone against the world, each one presents and declares itself. Don Duarte is the man of duty, even if he undertakes this duty unnecessarily against both his destiny and his country. Don Ferdinand asserts himself without fear in front of what is to come, "because whatever happens, it will / Never be bigger than (his) soul". John presents himself as the one who only knows how to desire "the entire sea, or the vain vanishing of the shores– / Either all, or nothing." And finally, concerning Don Sebastian, in regards to his grandiose and absurd enterprise, it becomes necessary that madness transmit itself to the world "with what was within it", to finally allow man to be something other than a "restrained cadaver which procreates". Even more similar to Pessoa, we find Don Pedro, this admirable stoic, who is the "dual master [...] Of duty and being", and who does not know how to divide himself in two: he retains the mastery of the dual question of being and duty. Through these deeply moving portraits the poet makes known his own dedication to the national destiny of Portugal. He thus publically displays the role he assumes and the part he plays.

Nonetheless there remains the price to pay for the adventure he proposes: during the first Discoveries, "so many mothers cried / so many sons prayed in vain!" The second "dispatch", "The Escutcheons" (Les Quines), hides nothing more than the glory that held the death of men and collective misfortunes as its counterpart. The poet's reply is that there is misfortune and bad luck. The worst misfortune, he claims, is that of the lucky, because "they are merely what is happening", satisfying themselves from what they have. To which he objects "life is brief and (that) the soul is vast", in such a manner that "to possess is to be late". All other misfortune is linked to the audacity of advancing into the unknown. It is a creative misfortune and, by consequence, of a "divine" essence, comparable to the suffering of Christ. From such a misfortune one must accept the risk: "Everything is worth it" the poet affirms, "once the soul is no longer small" ("Portuguese Sea").

## The reversal of the Portuguese landscape
The poem senses, within the fog of a vile époque where "people are lacking a soul", the return of the King Don Sebastian. From the heart of night, from within the storm, within the morning mist, the solemn call can emerge: "Now is the time". Assembled in order to form a small apologue, several poems via the story of three anonymous brothers clarify this figure of return. The vessel of the first brother drifts away "into the infinite sea"; the second brother departs to search within "the obscure fog"; neither one returning, the king refuses the third one to follow them. The first two brothers are nothing other than Power and Fame. With their disappearance, we also see depart "that which makes the soul heroic". It is not about believing that fame and power are at a hand's reach. It is better to expect nothing from such circumstances, but that the lively desire to achieve these attribute bears witness to the will to "find out who we are". A storm is brewing "beneath the sea":

Portugal stirs deep in its depths. Pessoa names this turbulence where he discerns a "desire of being capable of wanting": "being able to be". It is a subjective power of the possible present behind the appearances of stagnation and nothingness. Of course, the country is no more than a "bright, pallid earth", a "glow without fire or light"; it is the prey of an absolute disorientation, the absence of home and the abdication of any project whatsoever, which almost lead to its disappearance. But the poet wagers on a reversal: he affirms that it is possible to identify, within these negative traits, the "fog" of prophecy. He is the enunciator of the return of the disappeared king, forecasting a grandeur and universality whose site will once again be Portugal.

To make an effort for passage all the way to Isles of the Blessed, this place which "does not exist for the gaze", but where King Sebastian will have found refuge and from where he must return, is to uncover the existing "rupture" by which it will be possible to advance in the direction of truth. The Monster from the Confines of the Ocean, whose chimera terrified the seaman of the Discoveries, comes to be "called the one which sleeps today / And who was once Lord of the Sea". From his screams, he will wake a confusingly sleepy country from its nostalgia for the past and forgetful of its own universal vocation:

> Who is it that sleeps within memories
> Who unveils the Second World,
> And who does not want to unveil the Third?

The poem randomly asks for assistance: it hopes for the flash, the light of God, in order illuminate the darkness in which the country has plunged. If the legendary Ulysses was to engender Lisbon itself, he incarnates in the poem the possible rational figure of a sufficient national destiny for the country to maintain a consistency. Pessoa envisions that in circulating *Message*, its exposure to a decryption would render both intelligible the lamentable state within which a ruined Portugal lingers in anguish and dereliction, as well as its possible transmutation.

### Heteronymy, cosmopolitanism, universality
Just as the announcement of the emergence of a "Supra-Camoens" backed up his own transformation into a poet, the same can be said for the figure at the heart of *Message*. The figure of the hidden King, the Desired one, is the call to uncover what is hidden and encrypted (*encoberto*) within it. The poet hopes this reading will be the origin of a libratory and affirmative opening. The suffering one endures throughout *Message* comes from the fact that, for Pessoa, one perceives that nothing definitively takes place if its solitary effort does not announce the renaissance of the universality of an uncertain and obscure country where he lives:

> Alone feeling you and thinking you
> Fill and gild my empty days
> But when would you like to return?
> So, when then the King? And when the hour?

Neither his powerful poetic oeuvre nor the immense trajectory he accomplishes within the thought of the century has any intrinsic value to him whatsoever. Pessoa desperately wants his oeuvre to be the proof that the lost grandeur of Portugal can re-emerge, that his country will once again reveal itself capable of universality.

It is this hope which leads to the decision to publish
*Message* instead of *Fictions of the Interlude*. Jacinto do
Prado Coelho already remarked: "The subject of *Message*,
is not the Portuguese people nor concrete events, but the
essence of Portugal and the mission which it has to
accomplish." He compares Pessoa and Camoens
concerning this point, rightly calling both of them "poets of
absence. Poets of what was, or what could come to pass."[18]
Not at all the sycophants of the existing state of things. In
*Message*, the sequence of poems goes up against the sad
account of the negative signs of the present with the energy
and grandeur which were peculiar to several strong
subjectivities from the past. To present this book as a
nationalist hymn complying with the Salazarist vision of
the nation is not only the product of misinterpretation, but
truly forcing a counter-meaning. *Message* pursues in the
most vehement and brilliant fashion a proposition
completely at odds with what Salazar will allow to reign
during the long suffering decades. The lone grandeur
possible for Portugal will be to constitute itself as it did
during the époque of the Discoveries, as a site of the
universal. The poet maintains that this path is possible: his
poem has thought it, now it is up to the people to dare to
live it.

We shouldn't take this project to be a form of historical
megalomania in which the "national" would be nothing
more than an avatar of Pessoa, or an extension or annex of
his oeuvre. We are dealing, on the contrary, with a poet

---

[18] J. do Prado Coelho "Des *Luciades* à *Message* », in Actes du 1ᵉʳ Congrès d'études
pessoennes, Porto, Brazilia Editoro, Centro de Estudos Pessoanos, 1979, p. 308.

who addresses Portugal, its people, and his profound desire that the country may become a site of a heteronymy, which is to say, a multiplicity of truths. That all countries "wittingly and truthfully" exist within their own truths is the task Pessoa assigns to cosmopolitanism. For him, this cosmopolitanism resonates with what is most singular about Portugal: "The truly great act of Portuguese history – this long scientific and providential period of the Discoveries – is the grand cosmopolitan act of History." If the national, as it is represented in *Message*, sketches and projects this idea and denotes the capacity of a nation to possess in itself enough universality to be equivalent to the entire world, cosmopolitanism – no longer conceived as an empirical character of modern countries but as a conscious intellectual project – is its core: "Who thus, being Portuguese, can live within the narrowness of one personality, of one nation, of one faith?" asks the notes from 1923 (*Portugal between the past and future*). "We have already conquered the Sea"; from now on, we must "*be everything, in every way, because truth cannot exist if something is still missing.*" The idea of a multiple device, similar to the image of the heteronymy, here supports the vision of Portugal as a possible site of truth.

*Message* desperately attempts to rescue the lost greatness of Portugal and, in doing so, to recast the dice.

The decision to no longer publish while the *Estado Nova* of Salazar was in power acknowledges that the existence of this regime meant the failure of *Message*. The figure of the fold most hostile to the universal had won out. Don Sebastian did not return. But if the hidden King did not return, if Portugal did not notice and decipher the Message addressed to it, it is the poet who withdraws himself into a voluntary silence where death comes quickly to affix a final seal.

As Jacobson underlines in his magisterial analysis of the poem "Ulysses", ultimately "the poet deliberately leaves open the question of knowing if life on earth dies *in spite* of the intervention of the legend, or for lack of its intervention".[19] In this regard, in 1934, *Message* is a bet with the back against the wall. The pitch given in *Message* in regards to the *Fictions of the Interlude* or *The Book of Disquiet*, results from the desire to grasp a brief opportunity concerning the national. What had been decisive was to have attempted the intervention, going up against the risk of Portugal closing in upon the poet as if in a grave.

---

[19] Roman Jakobson, "Les oxymores dialectiques de Fernando Pessoa", in *Questions de poétique*, Paris, Editions du Seuil, coll. "Poétique", 1973, 2nd éd. rev. et corr., 1986, p. 474.

# 9
# The insubordination of the poem

> The poet is the one who always goes beyond what
> he is capable of doing.
>
> Fernando Pessoa

Heidegger is the first to identify the poem as the privileged
placeholder of the question of being. In an anti-Platonic
vision, he rehabilitates poets and poetry and returns the
verdict: to the being doomed to illusion, artifice, and
falsehood – their work, at least certain amongst them,
Hölderlin, Rilke, Trakl, George – is designated as the site
*par excellence* of truth in regards to being itself. This is
why the confrontation with the Pessoan heteronymy
imposes itself here.

In Heidegger, the privilege accorded these poets belongs to
a period of thought that he names, in renewing the terms of
Hölderlin, "a time of distress". It concerns an age "to which
we all still belong" and which the philosopher defines
thusly (in "What are poets for?", a fundamental text from
1946, announcing the 20th anniversary of Rilke's death,
published in *Basic Writings*[20]): "a time marked not only by

---

[20] The French title of Heidegger's book to which the author refers is *Chemins qui ne
mènent nulle part* (Paths which lead nowhere)

the distancing of God and departure of God, but the inability to retain this 'default of God' as a default." This God who has fled, is he the God of metaphysics? Must we read into his disappearance the sign of the "accomplishment of western metaphysics, Plato and Nietzsche included," its completion? Or are we heading in a direction, under this name of God, of the sacredness of Being which lends itself to operating, against metaphysics which has organized its own forgetting, a reversal, a return? Hölderlin, in any case, is the poet who knows, "singing, being attentive to the traces of the fleeing gods" ("What are poets for?"). The institution by Heidegger of a singular faceoff between the poet and the thinker is an internal decision proper to his vision of metaphysics and the history of philosophy: the occultation of the original gift of being by the constituent gesture of philosophy which distinguishes between Being and being (*être* and *étant*) and relegates being to its Idea as well as the organization of a forgetting of being by the entirety of western metaphysics are not considered errors, but belong to the destiny of being. Hölderlin intervenes in this history, whose course he himself interrupts, by the singular worry of the fleeing gods. Thus Heidegger can write "the countryside to which Hölderlin arrived is evidence of Being, which itself belongs to the destiny of Being; it is also starting with this destiny that this place is reserved to the poet" ("What are poets for?"). Hölderlin's poem is thus a site ("countryside" ...) whose existence is caught in a much vaster historicity, that of the destiny of Being within the history of western metaphysics.

The preeminence of the poem as a site of being is established in the work of Heidegger around being belonging to language. He says as much when he alternately declares it under the form of a general property of language: "Language is the dwelling of Being." ("What are poets for?"), or within a singular property which he names the Saying, and which is speech as much as it is the singular tongue of the poem: "The whole sphere of presence is present in the Saying" ("What are poets for?"). Heidegger forms this double thesis on the fact that the essence of language does not exhaust itself within meaning, nor can it be reduced to semantics or sign. Nonetheless, this thought of language, as the privileged site of Being, has no evidence whatsoever. Not even for poets, first, because for many of them, Being is rather what evades poetic speech, resists it. Heidegger is forced to reduce his overall theses concerning the relationship of language and Being as well as the presentation of presence and poetic saying, to a much more restrained thesis merely characterizing the poem as capable of the saying of being. At the same time he must isolate Rilke and Hölderlin amongst the poets. He then abandons the word "language" for the words "saying" and "the said", with which he will attempt to define the schema characteristic to language within the poem. Nevertheless, despite placing them aside, these theses continue to work clandestinely and establish the whole Heideggerian view of the poem.

"There is a Saying which expressly opens itself up to the Said as such, without pertaining to reasoning about language--which would also make it an object." "The entrance into a Said characterizes a Saying which follows a

trace of what is to be said, strictly in order to say it."
("What are poets for?")Such a Saying is a song. To sing the
song, for Heidegger, means to be present within the present
itself, to exist, to be capable of only doing this. But the
condition for the song to be as such is its remaining "a song
without speech". A song in which the "naming speech is
missing"("Hölderlin et l'essence de la poésie." In *Approche
de Hölderlin*). Hence the precariousness of the poetic
saying, according to Heidegger: "Speech, barely said,
escapes from the care of the poet, it cannot easily stand
firm in its truth, the knowledge of reserve funds and
economic proximity."("Return." In *Approche de Hölderlin*)
Hence, there is also the necessity to couple the Said with
"the naming speech", of instituting a confrontation between
the poet and the thinker.

Because, in fact, Heidegger's vision of the poem is split:
there is the "said" of the poem, but it is not the whole of the
poem. The poem bears more than its "said". And the task is
to "apprehend, by a sober and lucid thought, that which has
not been uttered within the "said" of the poem." ("What are
poets for?") Here we find again, as a counter-relief, the old
re-presentation of the poet as a figure of drunkenness, who
does not possess, who does not know what he says even
though he says it.

Furthermore, how is it that something which is not uttered
in the poem can nonetheless be there within the poem? It is
via the analysis of the poems of Rilke that Heidegger put
his own thought to the test. The fundamental words of this
poet, he maintains, "may only be understood within the
region from where they have been uttered." Regarding

Rilke, Heidegger advances the idea, that "this region" is the "essence of being" since the completion of western metaphysics by Nietzsche." And yet, "the sphere from which these poems speak (the Elegies and the Sonnets) is not yet sufficiently thought starting from the essence of metaphysics itself." Heidegger calls for constructing a mastery of "the genuine nature of poetry" and of thought in order for a dialogue between poetry (Dichten) and thought (Denken) to be possible. The ultimate point of this meditation is this: one must be capable of arriving to the point where "a poetic saying can also be the oeuvre of a thought". Against the previous opposition of poem/thought, a thinking and poetic interiority would be a new necessary hypothesis: "This is what still remains for us to understand." ("What are poets for?") .

In this text Heidegger has laid out two grand inaugural figures: a node between the poem and Time (a singular modality of the historical ties between being and Time) and a one-on-one (vis-à-vis) between the poem and thought, hesitating between an affirmation of the necessity for the poem to have a speech external to its saying (a poem showing what it possesses without knowing it), and a thought which would be completely internal to the poem.

The poem plays an essential role in the reversal which occurred within the fate of being: "The poets are those mortals whom, solemnly singing of the wine god, sense the trace of the flight of the gods, and remain on their trail, and trace, for their mortal brethren, the path of reversal." ("What are poets for?")

The poem orients thought: "The poet thinks towards the location which determines itself through the beginning of the clearing of Being which, as the figure of self-completion of western metaphysics, began to take its own form." ("What are poets for?")

From then on, the poem find itself lead into thinking the thought that it is: "these poets must expressly say within their poetic saying the essence of poetry." "Thus, condition of the poet and poetic vocation becomes the question." ("What are poets for?")

To be more exact, Heidegger is neither concerned with the poem and Time, the poem and thought, nor with the poem and the thought of the poem, but with the *poet* and Time, the *poet* and thought, the *poet* and the essence of poetry. This culminates in Heidegger designating Hölderlin as "the poet's poet" ("Hölderlin and The Essence of Poetry"). The poem as such is subordinate either to language considered as the dwelling of Being, or to the metaphysical site which determines what the poem contains without saying it, or to the figure of the poet, when it is – in the case of Hölderlin -, the bearer of the *historial* essence of poetry.

Today the question of being has fallen into oblivion: these words, found in the opening pages of *Being and Time*, would no doubt have been heard by Pessoa with force. To raise the question of Being in order to once again reform the central question concerning thinking, and that this opens a radical critique of metaphysics – is this not an analysis the master of the heteronyms shares with Heidegger?

For this German philosopher, the essence of all metaphysical thinking is to submit two unequal, antithetical instances of Being: of distinguishing "that which truly is" and "that which truly is not" ("Who is the Zarathustra of Nietzsche?" in *Essays and Conferences*). Couplings of essence and appearance, object and subject, of the thing-in-itself and the thing-for-itself, of being and non-being, etc. The omnipresence of duality, in his eyes, is more important, more fundamental than the terms that name them. For the Keeper, metaphysics prevents thought from relating to things as things; it makes of being a background of the thing; and of the thing, the point of departure for an interpretation.

The philosopher and the poet both share the analysis according to which metaphysics, making being an object, reduces the thinking of being to a problem of knowledge, to the question of deciding if thinking, separated from the object, can still be a thinking of the real. Against metaphysics, they both attempt to return to a pre-Platonic thinking of Being and, to be more precise, a return to Parmenides, searching for the new conditions under which it is possible to reiterate the affirmation: "thinking and being are the same".

This "same", denoting the mode in which thought is a part of being, presents itself as an enigma to Heidegger, and it is in order to clarify it that he makes a detour by the hypothesis of the "Greek-being" of language. The essence of language revels itself within the "saying" (*Sage*), and this "saying" has its singularity not only in an arranging of a "letting-something-spread out" which is logos, language, or discourse, but also a "making manifest", or *physis*, which is the world, which is being, as it appears. ("Moira" ("Parménide VIII", *34-41*), in *Essais et Conférences*) Thinking the identity of being and thought was made possible by this dual capacity of the "saying" – a capacity which, according to the philosopher, only perpetuates itself as such within the poem. Every thinking of being raised against the forgetting of being must bind itself with poetry as a saying [Gedicht]. And it is within the poem of Hölderlin that Heidegger discovers an authentic saying of being.

This vision establishes a strong ambivalence in the relationship between Heidegger and poetry. The poem is essential because what it has to think, "the sameness" of thinking and being, finds itself carried away by the poetic saying. But if Being is originally veiled, it is not merely because metaphysics forgets about it behind being, but also because it finds itself buried within language. This mode of double presence of Being within language pushes Heidegger, in a same movement, to turn towards the poem and deny it the capacity of being the thought of its saying. "[...] There must first be men who are thinkers, so that the speech (parole) of the poet becomes perceptible." ("Return") It is the philosopher, or rather the thinker, who will think Being which poems conceal without knowing. In this sense, the interpretation is consubstantial with Heidegger's relationship with the poem. Because the poem does not know what it says. It says, without saying what it says. It ignores that it is the identity of both thinking and being.

This thought is still amenable to the critique of metaphysics performed by the Keeper. The eye of the philosopher indeed remains the one which Caeiro challenges: "This particular eye – this eye not for what it sees, but for what we have already within our sight when we see what we see – not everyone has this eye", writes Heidegger. "In order to have it, one must have the capacity to distinguish between *what reveals itself from oneself*, or opens itself up following its own deployment, *and what does not reveal itself from oneself*" ("What is and what determines the Physis", in *Questions II*). The movement that consists of forsaking being in order to "look all the way into Being" is devoid of any signification (*sens*) for the Keeper. For him, there is no Being which would be "the truth of Being". Nor for that matter a "Nature" which would be this truth, nor any "beauty" of the poem which would be the presence, somewhat unconscious of itself, of this true Being.

In Heidegger, the thought of "being as such" is substituted for the idea of being as gift. This thought exists under the condition that the affirmation of a "there is" (*il y a*) liberates Being from its withdrawal, rips it away from its veiling by being. It is concerning this exact point that the question of Time comes to articulate itself with that of Being: the dual movement of withdrawal and the ripping away from this withdrawal constitutes an arrival of the "present in presence" and thus creates a temporality. Time imposes itself as an intrinsic dimension of Being, which is buried within the said, and of access to Being which is necessarily given as a return. The "same" of Parmenides thus becomes, in Heidegger, "temporal". Eternity as a trait of Being, independence, –which belongs as much to

essences and to the Supreme Being as well as to the Idea –
are for him, in regards to Time, guiding ideas of
metaphysics and must be dismissed. We know, however,
that Caeiro does not want time "in his plan", because for
him Being, from the outset is entirely given within things.
In the poetry of the Keeper, there is neither presence of the
present nor arrival of Being to presence, but merely an
eternal present, if we dare risk this oxymoron, that is to say,
a present without time.

That "all metaphysics, including its counterpart, positivism,
speaks the language of Plato" ("The end of Philosophy and
the Task of Thought" *in Questions IV*), is a thesis which
Caeiro will grant Heidegger. In order to battle or bypass
metaphysics, and more specifically its Platonic matrix,
Heidegger and the Keeper resort to the poem: in one case to
the poem as "saying" and, in the other case, the poem as
"seeing".

Caeiro proposes the gaze-thought of the poem as an
imminent site of the identity of thinking and being, while
for Heidegger, the poem is a sort of "unconscious" site of
Being, and its truth must be deciphered from the outside. In
the work of the Keeper, the poem only exceeds
metaphysics by its special ability of inventing new
operations and figures of thought, while for Heidegger, it is
designated as a type of linguistic resource within which
Being is enclosed, the operation of the uncovering of Being
within the poem left to the thinker and not the poet:
"Language (Sprache) is the initial dimension within which
man-being can correspond to (entsprechen) being and its
demand, and within corresponding to it belongs to being.

This initial correspondence, accomplished on its own, is thought" ("The Turning", in *Questions IV*).

The Pessoan heteronymy treats the sequence of the crisis of metaphysics and its overcoming as a singular situation for poetry. An open and multiple apparatus, centered upon *The Keeper of Sheep*, will be made from it and indeed will lead to a critique of the metaphysics internal to the poem at the same time maintaining a "metaphysics without metaphysics". Heidegger tackles the question from the point of view of the history of philosophy and via the historical figure of Being. In the first instance, the poem thinks being and, within the heteronymous multiplicity of poems, the thinking which it is. In the second instance, the poem waits for a thinker external to it, whom would uncover the truth which it unwittingly contains within its withdrawal: "It is only when man as 'Shepherd of Being' encounters the truth of being as something for which he must take responsibility, that he can expect the coming of the destiny of Being [...]" ("The Turning").

Divergences and proximities between philosopher and poet are definitively concentrated around the opposition of the "Shepherd of Being" and the "Keeper of Sheep".

## The Heideggerian interval and the Pessoan interval

The essence of the poet Hölderlin, according to Heidegger, exists between the Time of the fugitive gods and the god still to come. "Is god alive or does he remain dead?" Such is the question the thinker poses to the poet, because: "If god is god, he comes from the constellation of being and from its interior" ("The Turning"). Doing away with philosophy in order to do away with metaphysics (or doing away with metaphysics in order to do away with philosophy) has as a corollary in Heidegger the return of the figure of the sacred. Thus, the overcoming of metaphysics does not mean a renunciation of theology, but a return to it by a retrograde movement, because metaphysics first and foremost had been a rejection of the sacred, an attempt to rationally think the existence of God. Furthermore, what the language of the poet bears must pass by the intermediary of the thinker "in the Occidental language of the Germans" in order to make itself heard. This assignment of the thinking of Being to a national site recalls the German history as fate. This interval between time periods apprehends the poem not as an interlude between two different metaphysical states, but as a bridge between theology and history.

In doing this, by creating a path comparable to the one Pessoa sketches out in *Message* does Heidegger borrow from him: in arranging, beginning with the poem, an essence of the national in which the future of the country plays itself out? The temporal proximity of the two undertakings is striking: *Message* published in 1934; Heidegger's essay, *Hölderlin and the Essence of Poetry*, in 1936. Moreover, for the German philosopher as for the Portuguese poet, the deliverance by the poem of a national essence implies a figure of Return – a return to the native land (Hölderlin), a return of the disappeared king (Don Sebastian, The Desired). Both of them wager on the possible meeting between the poetic work and the collective national subjectivity. Both equally strive for an equation which would be the identifying singularity of the country, a vocation detectable via the past. And the deciphering of the language of the poet holds a central role in the constitution of a new national subjectivity. Nonetheless, within each one of these shared points, they once again differ and disagree.

Heidegger thinks himself capable, starting with Hölderlin's poetry, of enouncing that the return "is the step which heads towards the proximity of origins" and that "the best and most secret part of the homeland relies in this: to be only this proximity to origins and nothing else" ("Return").

Dreadful words when they are accompanied with the conviction that this origin is nothing less than the "historial Being of the Germans". On the other hand, there is no such problem about origin at work in *Message*. What is in question here is clearly the capacity of a universality to find its way to the present. This does not mean to re-summon myth as national origin, but to separate it into its rational part which it would strive to activate and its legendary part which vanishes and dies, once the rational utterance has been identified and transmitted by the poem.

Concerning the encounter between the poet and a collective subjectivity, Heidegger calls for a fusion: "If those 'whose anxieties are about the homeland' become the Anxious in an essential manner, there is thus an alliance with the Poet. There is thus a return. And this return is the future of the *historial* being of the Germans" ("Return"). Thus, it is outrageous to assign to Germany as a political figure ("those who are anxious about the homeland") the privilege of being the unique site of the return of the thinking of being. Here, we have a fusion and confusion of the political and the poetical.

When Pessoa proposes the deciphering of *Message*, he is, on the contrary, searching for a principle of displacing the national outside the political sphere. He makes the wager that a mobilized collective subjectivity within a nationalist disposition can be displaced, that the national disposition can be re-oriented by the poem towards a voluntary universalism, reviving the intellectual grandeur of the Portugal of the Discoveries and rejecting its imperial, material, and terrestrial power.

Heidegger maintains the constituting utterance of the "national" in Germany is the following: "The Germans are the people of the Poem *and* Thought" ("Return"). Thus, for him the national is substantive in a people. The philosopher thus decrees a superiority of the German site as an eminent site of the thinking of Being which will succeed philosophy and metaphysics. Germany is the lone nation which can make it so that the ontological language of the poet can be heard. "Germany" is thus the name of the site where the withdrawal of being will be both thought and overcome. Pessoa, however, in *Message*, will not substantiate any people whatsoever. Via Portuguese history, he will highlight the few figural bearers of a universalism. "Portugal" is the name for a possible location of a universality which is itself open and multiple. The Portugal, encrypted by *Message*, exemplifies a universalist figure of the national more than incarnating one.

For Heidegger, Hölderlin's importance comes from the fact that he is the "poet's poet". In the sense, that he "poetizes" the essence of poetry. From the interior of a time, which is a time of distress because metaphysics has deprived it of any access whatsoever to being, Hölderlin has rebuilt poetry as the site of the truth of being. In continuity with what Philippe Lacoue-Labarthe analyzes as a "certain German tradition resulting from Romanticism", Heidegger thinks the organization of a national community can only be achieved by concentrating itself around an artistic figure. Hölderlin, master of a grand German ontological art, would be the figure to found the existence of a German people.

Pessoa equally presents Caeiro as rebuilding the essence of poetry. But from Caeiro to *Message*, there is no continuity whatsoever, no link. It is not Caeiro's founding ontological innovation which supports the singular proposition of the national contained within *Message*. All of the heteronymy is dissenting to any sort of politics, but the same can also be said for *Message*. Furthermore, there is no link at all established by Pessoa between the heteronymous poetic overhaul of the relations between the poem to philosophy and to metaphysics, and the question of the national. Here, we are not dealing with fusing an oeuvre and the creation of a people. We are talking about the establishment, via the poem, and the eventual deciphering via the country, of a singular concept of universality. Pessoa is as far away from the idea that his poem, like Heidegger says, would constitute all by itself "as the poetic oeuvre as such, the return itself". (A return, which in the case of Hölderlin's oeuvre, "continues to take place as long as its speech resonates within the language of the Germans".)

## Metaphysics, ontology, philosophy, and poem

The imperious and salvatory return to the poem introduces in Heidegger, as far as philosophy is concerned, quite the tremor. In order for the possibility to think being anew, does it mean we must put an end to philosophy? Does thinking being demand another type of thought other than philosophy? This is precisely what is argued once philosophy and metaphysics are identified with each other: if the core of philosophy is metaphysics, if metaphysics and philosophy overlap each other and coincide, then thinking being must demand something other than philosophy, since metaphysics which is at the heart of it, renders access to being impossible. But sometimes Heidegger is more inclined towards the idea that philosophy has been placed outside of itself, outside of its proper path, by its metaphysical orientation and has abandoned its essential grounding which was a thinking of Being. The hesitation concerning this point reverberates around the figure of origin: must we count Parmenides amongst the poets? Or should we count him as one of the first philosophers, borrowing from the poem the gesture of banning a path and prescribing another? Bypassing the Platonic apparatus obligates Heidegger to articulate other connections between poetry and philosophy besides that of reciprocal exclusion. In the end, it's the Heideggerian *historial* montage – the adhesion of the figure of Being to Time, its deployment within a historical time whose philosophies are major events – which demands a destitution of philosophy, closing and hardening the initial hypothesis. Within this vision of things, against the veiling made by metaphysics, the "saying" alone of the poem can act. There is a heavy price to pay, beginning with the impossibility of establishing a thinking of being without subordinating the poem. Poets – certain poets: Rilke, Hölderlin, Trakl – are proclaimed as the "champions" of the question of being, against the organizing philosophy of its forgetting.

If in a certain manner, the work of the German philosopher, like the Portuguese poet, begins with the refusal of the idea that the thinking of Being can be reduced to a theory of knowledge, Heidegger assigns this configuration of metaphysics to what he calls "modern philosophy", while for Pessoa, it is above all else a sequence in which "within philosophy, something has been lost". The philosopher concludes that not only should we end philosophy due to its responsibility towards the forgetting of Being, we should substitute in its place a thinking which would have as its essential task to make heard what in the poem continues to allow for Being to appear beyond its withdrawal. Philosophy can only be destitute because it first had been completely identified with metaphysics: "Philosophy means metaphysics", writes Heidegger without hesitation (*The End of Philosophy and the Task of Thinking*). To replace philosophy with a thinking which does not give itself the name of ontology but stitches itself to the poem to, in the end, find access to Being is quite an ambiguous operation. Thus the poem finds itself subordinate to a thinking that thinks it from the outside, to the extent that it would contain, without knowing it, the truth of Being. Moreover, this apparatus upholds the question of Being within the field of the question of truth, even if it proposes a radical mutation of the category of Truth.

Heidegger subordinates the poet and the poem to the advent of a thought whose exteriority to philosophy does not guarantee that its last resort is not onto-theological. The heteronymy substitutes for this split between thought and the poem a multiple poetic apparatus in which poetry thinks *poetry as a possible transitory thinking of Being*, within a tight faceoff with metaphysics and philosophy.

By his virulent critique of metaphysics, Caeiro sustains the nearest and at the same time the greatest distance from the German philosopher. The orthonym meditates on the possibility of a nihilism linked to the collapse of metaphysics, but he also introduces the thinking of Being as fiction and the affirmation of a radical disassociation between the thinking of Being and the thinking of truths. Reis explores the necessity of pushing the thinking of Being all the way to the question of existence and thus temporality. Articulating that thinking, not existence, distinguishes the being of man amongst things, he nevertheless rejects the path of Heidegger of subordinating Being itself to time. Campos, in appearance a poet of excess and anxiety, is actually the most prudent and moderate to the extent that he does not admit that Caeiro's position of mastery within the heteronymy would be capable of constituting poetry as the successor to philosophy.

Thus heteronymous poetry does not enact the end of metaphysics; it critiques its dualities. It is not the successor of philosophy; it wittingly assumes ontology, thus testing poetry's capacity of thinking Being.

Working with the hypothesis that the poem can bear a "metaphysics without metaphysics", the heteronymy distinguishes and separates ontology and philosophy. It distributes ontology upon the poetic heteronymy and places this poetic ontology outside the field of Truth, at the same time, moreover, leaving open and outside its reach the questions of Truth and the becoming of philosophy.

The heteronymous "method" is exhaustion: each one of the poets goes to the end of the thought which he is, after which, he stops. This compactness makes each one of these oeuvres an intense poetic unit. Furthermore, it obliges one to acknowledge the existence of discontinuities within thought and, more precisely, the ontological discontinuities between the four poets.

Thus the heteronymy is also a prodigious lesson concerning the poem as materiality. It is an absolutely materialist thinking of the poetic procedure.

Contrary to what Heidegger affirms,[21] the figures from the poem are not linguistic figures. They are, according to our originating hypothesis, *thought figures* (*figures de pensée*). It is within the gap between saying and the linguistic tongue – an effect of the violence that the former exerts on the latter – that a "thought figure" appears within the poem. The thought figure is not a figure *of thought*, nor *thought turned into figures*. It is a new element produced by the poem, and to seize upon it is to each time demand a non-

---

[21] All the quotes from Heidegger in this chapter are taken from *"Chemins qui mènent nulle part*, Paris, Gallimard, 1962; *Approche de Hölderlin*, Paris, Gallimard, 1962 and 1973; *Essais et Conférences* Paris, Gallimard, 1968; *Questions II*, Paris, Gallimard, 1968; *Questions IV*, Paris, Gallimard, 1976.

interpretative grasp of the poem. The heteronymy affirms an essential insubordination of the poem.

# 10
# A positive figure of nonachievement

*Message* failed, and *Fictions of the Interlude* did not see the light of day: the oeuvre of the four poets remains in a state of an unfinished construction site. What is it then that allows for the imperative of an opening?

The strength of the heteronymous invention resides in it being entirely poetic, being the "heteronymous web" of four great poets.

Pessoa, fiercely highlighting the fact that the heteronymy is an apparatus belonging to literature and, because of this fact, foreign to philosophy, indicates that if the heteronymy does not allow itself be composed as a system, it should nonetheless not be taken as an expression of skepticism:

> The confection of these works does not indicate a state of metaphysical opinion. What I mean is that in totalizing in writing these "aspects" of reality within persons who are their beholders, I am not proposing a philosophy which would insinuate that nothing real exists with the exception of "aspects which are imprisoned" by a reality – which would itself be illusory or non-existent. No, I have neither this philosophical belief nor its contrary belief. From within my own field of mastery, which is literature, I am a professional in the best sense of the word. Which is to say, I am scientific worker who does not authorize opinions which are foreign to the literary

specialization to which he has devoted himself. And the fact that I do not have such a philosophical opinion nor its contrary opinion, in regards to these "book-persons", nevertheless should not induce the thought that I am a skeptic. (Text, presumed to be from 1930, published in *Textos escritos para projectados prefacios ao livro 'Ficçoes do Interludio'*).

Why is the heteronymy not a system? The poet replies: because it should not be confused with a "state of metaphysical opinion", for example with the Kantian critique of the real. What is presented or borne by the heteronymous individualities within the interior of literature cannot be interpreted as a pre-existing philosophical opinion.

Above all, the heteronymy separates and fragments. The mode of affirmation proper to it is demarcation (*délimitation*). Against a certain poetic tradition, it separates the poem from metaphysics. From within the interior of itself, it distinguishes between the project of a metaphysics without metaphysics (Caeiro's oeuvre), and a non-metaphysical ontology (the group of the four heteronyms). On its outer edge, it disjoints the poetic ontology and philosophy. In the end, it demarcates the processes in which thinking being is at stake of those which demand a thinking of truths. Concerning each one of these points, the Pessoan heteronymy effectuates a powerful clarification which is its own figure of freedom.

It is possible to capitulate around what the "thinking thought" positions itself in looking at five great questions: what the poem articulates in regards to the relationship between the poem and metaphysics; what is the location or the "site" of the poem; what does the poem orchestrate as the task of the poem; what are the poetic procedure(s) which characterize it; what is the mode in which the demarcation between poem and philosophy is produced.

## The general outline of the heteronymy

Caeiro has the responsibility of separating the poem from metaphysics and rendering the onto-theology linked to it useless.

This separation is produced within the transformation of the poem itself, following the innovations which are proposed by the Keeper. The poem must become the site of a thinking instructed in seeing. Or better still, a "non-thinking" in opposition to what it is to think being, the world, and the universe within the metaphysical field.

There is a rupture, a desire of breakdown, represented by Caeiro as splitting the history of poetry: for the first time, the poem deals with its own criteria as far as it wants to relate non-metaphysically with the being of the world and the universe.

It is not a reflexive but immanent process: the poem strives to deeply modify itself as a poem. It becomes the poem of the act of seeing, of things, of prose, against expressivity, the ulterior-motive, dual meanings.

The poem argues against philosophy the possibility of a metaphysics without metaphysics. The eminent task confided to the poem is, against philosophy, to "keep" ontology. This is how the poet justifies his name as the "Keeper".

Next, we have Campos.

For him, the main imperative shifts: it is no longer about interrupting metaphysics but deciding if one should or should not exit romanticism and if this is truly possible.

The location of the poem remains romanticism. By his attention to the multiple, to the instability of "what is happening", this seems for Campos to be the lone activity capable of intervening within the matrixial Platonic reverie of any poem. He attempts to saturate this site, to establish within it a distance, in using the romantic poem as a "primary material" for his own poem.

The loss, or the undoing of metaphysics, is thought by him to be as much provisory as effective. The poem must watch over the perpetuation of metaphysical emotion as long as no metaphysical project seems possible, since none of them are viable except waiting for another invention.

The poem of Campos does not produce, properly speaking, innovations: it effectuates crossings of the different possible metaphysical sites. In doing this, he produces a double figure of exhaustion of the romantic poem: one could say that he attempts to exit via the high ("Odes" and millimetric poems) and from the low (discouraged poems).

Philosophers are neither outcast nor sidelined by Campos. On contrary, the poem undertakes fraternal and melancholic discussions with them. From within the interior of its confrontation with philosophy and metaphysics, *this poet is a Watchman* (*veilleur*).

Reis, who wants to be the closest disciple to Caeiro, stiffens or partially warps the thought-poem of the Keeper.

He takes as his departure the certainty that a new poetic ontology exists which explains itself within the oeuvre of the master.

He has set for himself the extension of the ontology of the Keeper who pronounces, via a thinking of Being as things, the absolute contingency of everything.

To endure this contingency demands some sort of wisdom – a thinking of existence as such – and an ethics – allowing it to pass from contingency to eternity.

The spirit of this ethics comes from aesthetics: the poem as pure form molded upon the idea.

The ethico-ontologico rupture introduced by the poem of the Keeper "splits in two" the history of poetry. It also splits in two the history of men, in the sense that it authorizes doing away with any vision of gods as primary and supreme instances of Being. Since Reis patiently turns them into fiction, *the extreme greatness of this poet comes from the fact that he can be called the Eraser of the gods.*

Finally, the orthonym is the one who evades the mastery of Caeiro.

For this poet, metaphysics is not only broken, but impossible. This end of metaphysics results from its own deficiencies; it is not an effect from the critique produced by the poem.

The lone thing of which the poem is capable is providing the ability of seeing the undecidability of being and non-being, of establishing and repeating the nihilistic quadrature of non-being, of nothing, of the void and nothingness.

The ethics of the poem is to show that any articulation concerning being is outside the category of truth. Around being and non-being, the poem can eventually construct fiction. Thus, this poet is above all a "Fictioneer" (*fingidor*).

That the poet is a Fictioneer leaves in suspense the question of knowing if the poem can be "truth and a path" or if it only ever stenographs nothingness.

Its metaphysical core being not only broken but dead, every philosophy is futile, every philosophy is just as good as another. Philosophy is foreign to the poem, or it is itself, "poems".

## The power of the heteronymous delimitation

The heteronymous invention is so powerful that it can indeed endure several interpretations. Whether these are phenomenological – privileging the figures of a shattered consciousness, of a subjective loss of identity, of a desire of dissimulation – or formalist – insisting on language games, inter-textuality, the multiplicity of writings – they nevertheless do not address the question itself of knowing what the heteronymy thinks.

The double birth of the heteronymy, fictions of characters and lives of poets, staged debates and polemics at the heart of the *Family Discussion,* attempts to create with the figure of Antonio Mora a "heteronymous philosopher", some sort of stance within their poems of the disciples in regards to their master: we find here so many attempts on behalf of Pessoa himself, as Mallarmé's expression goes, "of thinking his own thought".

The heteronymy constitutes a proposition concerning poetry as a thought of poetry as thinking. The doubling here is essential: it first indicates that this thinking concerning the poem is a thinking which is immanent to the poem. Poetry as thinking about itself to the extent that it purports itself to be a thought. But what does this thought think?

The heteronymy affirms that a task of the poem exists with regards to metaphysics and that this task is two-fold. The poem must both radically critique metaphysics and continue to bear its ambition.

It must critique its duality, which is to say the separation which metaphysics establishes (since Plato) between the thing or object and thought or essence, between phenomenon and consciousness – and then posing the problem of knowing as a difficult or impossible relation between the two terms. To this duality, Caeiro pits the conviction of a profound homogeneity between things and thought: on the one hand, because thought, within the poem, can become capable of seeing them as things, but also because there is not a decisive difference between thought and things. One could also put it this way: there is no *Dasein* for Caeiro. Thus, thinking being remains possible within the interior of the poem. Here we find the master's challenge.

In Caeiro, in as much as it influences the poem, metaphysics is negatively identified. The critique of the Keeper must be by itself, within an innovative figure, a poetic critique of the poem. This immanence from the critique to the metaphysician poem is the ultimate reason of Caeiro's mastery. His project can be described as a *"metaphysics without metaphysics"*, or a distinct poetic ontology. The poem has as its task to release poetry from metaphysics – it's the oeuvre of the "gaze-thought" removed from the metaphysical mode of thinking – it must also fight for ontology against philosophy. Only a *poetic* ontology would have the strength of being a non-metaphysical ontology. However, in order to achieve this task, Caeiro's oeuvre is not enough: for a poetic ontology to form, one needs the ensemble of the four poets, one needs the heteronymy itself.

In Campos, the poetic critique of metaphysics presents itself as being less self-assured. Campos is not sure the poem can be the successor of philosophy. This doubt shows itself within a hesitation of departing from the romantic configuration. The stumbling block is the question of the infinite. Is the poem capable not only of thinking things and the multiple, but of forming a non-onto-theological (or also a non-romantic) thinking of the infinite? In Campos, all the paradigms of the infinite are intra-physical: desire and movement, speed and energy. In this way, his poem reproduces natural figures of the infinite, rather than providing new ones. Failing, concerning this point, to expand a non-metaphysical ontology, Campos' poem chooses to save metaphysics in trying to *perpetuate the emotion* of it.

Reis takes as his departure the conviction that the rupture with metaphysics has been produced and that the oeuvre of the Keeper holds all the keys of a non-metaphysical ontology. He does not, as Campos does with the infinite, elaborate new questions; nor does he imagine, as the orthonymous non-disciple, that the thinking of things cannot substitute for a thinking of non-being. If Campos incarnates the figure of the rebellious disciple, Reis, on the other hand, expresses that of the fascinated disciple whose tragic obsession is to conform his life, even up to his being itself, to the consequences of a thinking which troubles and disturbs him. This is also the reason why his thought is in part the dogmatic reorientation and hardening of the Keeper's oeuvre. Its strength is to nonetheless know how to expose itself without reservation to the consequences.

Contrary to Reis, the orthonym could be defined as refusing to endorse the interrupting character of Caeiro-thought: he excludes any possibility of an uplifting of metaphysics by the poem. This disclaimer, for as much as it nonetheless works from the interior of the existence of Caeiro's poem, from the interior of the thinking of being as things, creates a new demarcation whose consequences are considerable: the refusal that any thinking of being can establish itself within the register of a *truth* of being. For the poem, to think being is not to say being as truth, but on the contrary, to expose its structure as fiction.

### Orientations and not Totalizations

Heteronymous ontological thinking is thus a thinking without unity. It is not the same poetic operations which allow for the thinking that being is things; that being and non-being are not in a relation of a dialectical procreation, but within an inextricable dual co-existence; that the infinite, being in excess to being, cannot be thought starting from the finite nor from natural paradigms; or what are the ethical maxims of which this ontology consists. *It is because they are not same operations that they are not the same poems.* And because they are not the same poems, they cannot come from the same poets. Not only is the thought localized – always springing forth from some point, or location – but it must *show* that it is located as such. It has to break away from any appearance of unity and, on the contrary, construct, via a powerful fiction, discontinuity. This is the price for an innovative ontological capacity of the poem.

If the heteronymy is in a position to take the place of metaphysics, it is under the condition that it proves itself capable of establishing a new configuration of what we can call thinking when we are dealing with what it is to think being. This is great question that the establishing gesture of the Keeper, assigning being to things and thinking without metaphysics to the gaze-thought, does not entirely resolve. The heteronymous solution is to create a field within which thinking neither proceeds by repetition nor totalization, but by successive orientations. This is what the figures of the master, the two unequal disciples and the opponent bearing the "right name" materialize. The heteronymy thus guides the affinities of the poem, metaphysics, philosophy, and ontology. In traversing this network, it becomes possible to think these affinities as an entirely novel situation of *the poem itself.*

That which does not fall within ontology, nor metaphysical anguish – love, politics, history, the question of the national – finds itself removed, not necessarily outside the field of poetry, but outside the field of the heteronymy as such. Love occupies a singular place because it in a way puts the poetic ontology to the test. This is the question upon which the poems of the *Shepherd in Love* meditate: within love are we still dealing with being, the thinking of being? And if this is not the case, what is this thought then which is love?

There is an exception for love, and an innovation as far as politics are concerned: the denial, present in each one of these four poets, that politics can be internal to poetry, goes with the affirmation that this thinking demands an attention and proper procedures, to which Pessoa will moreover consecrate, outside of the poem, quite a bit of his time and intellect.

The heteronymy in prose of *The Book of Disquiet* is a "semi"-heteronymy because it introduces within the heteronymy a phenomenology. This book makes of metaphysics not so much a thinking but an experience. Wherever a poem proceeds via an affirmation (specifically the heteronymous poem), Soares' thinking progresses by interruptions and repetitions. His method is much more a questioning than a fragmenting.

Not being able to think being, that things can elude thought instead of peacefully existing within a space of reverie and vision: this is what the little office employee metaphysician experiences each day. All he needs is the city, its houses, the moon, the boss Vasques, the grocery clerk, the fruit merchant, in order for the question of existence to emerge from "what there is" and the question of reality from "what there isn't". Metaphysics survives within the obscurity of Rua dos Douradores. There it will eternally remain because it inhabits as much blind disquietude of anonymous people as it does the peremptory writings of philosophers and poets.

The grandeur of Pessoa's "Faust" who is also a figure plagued by the impasses of metaphysics, a figure of the impossible mourning of philosophy, of the critical wandering, is to incarnate, next to the poetic heteronymy, the persistence of an indefinitely pensive thinking. The existence of this dramatic play, itself incomplete, highlights the scale of *passion* Pessoa has for metaphysics – a passion which is capable of generating a resolvent poetic configuration, the heteronymy, and to continue parallel to it within the aporia. It is as if, by this gigantic and multiform effort, the poet strives to inhabit *all* the subjective sites of the crisis.

Thus the poetic heteronymy is not transverse to all that the poet thinks. It contents itself – and this is considerable – with positively untangling the crisis of the poem, making it pass through critical paralysis to thinking of its situation and to its own capacities.

### Dissemination and localizations
The heteronymy is homogeneous, within its formal apparatus, to the ontology which it declares it bears. Indeed, it evades interpretation. It only proposes plurality and multiplicity; in principle, there exists merely emptiness

and inconsistency; the author himself is here an evanescent figure; and yet even more striking, within it, there is no longer "the" poet, but "poets". The heteronymy resists interpretation because it resists totalization. It presents a heterogeneous multiplicity which, according to Caeiro, renders it identical to Nature: in the image of it (Nature), it is "parts without a whole".

It is this heterogeneity internal to the heteronymy which authorizes the poem to not only bear a thinking of *poetry*, but a thinking of *poetry as thought*.

Fictitious but not factitious, the poetic heteronymy differentiates via the poem the thinking of being and the thinking of truths.

Indeed, the poetic heteronymy does not think from within the category of truth. The metaphysical dualities (the couplings of mind/matter, reality/appearance, presence/absence, consciousness/real, subject/object, or interpretation/mystery) root themselves within an indexing of being to truth. It is always about saying the truth of being, which supposes that the being of Being and the being of Truth are fused together. All these figures of truth – whether they give themselves up to the adequacy of being and thought, which is the case within classical metaphysics, or within the withdrawal and the forgetting of being as in Heidegger – correspond to figures of being as carriers of meaning and sense.

The heteronymous ontology assumes a character of being that is completely devoid of meaning and sense: fragmented presentation and the structuring of fictions are consequences. The heteronymous corpus is no more unified in its poetic operations than mathematics. Or rather, a heteronymous "corpus" does not exist: the incompleteness and fragmentation proves that the heteronymous ontology, as soon as it strives to deploy a thinking of being removed from truth and meaning, finds itself subjected to disseminations and localizations.

This immense attempt of thinking being non-metaphysically in the guise of the poem – which is another possible summarization of the heteronymy – in the end, can only offer or construct fictional structures: fiction of the four poets, fiction of the "family discussion", poet as fictioneer, fiction of the gods and the Keeper. Pessoa, who had wanted to be a severe critic of metaphysics, discovers how, from within the interior of this fabulous multiple poetic ontology where each heteronymous poet is a territory, he can also be a "courier": Courier and not merely a by-stander, not at all the remarkable by-stander which Mallarmé anointed Rimbaud. And yet, a by-stander, Pessoa surely was, often being photographed strolling in Lisbon, as well as through his own life. Nevertheless, his own greatness is that of passing through: neither program nor promise, a decisiveness of ensuring a crossing, and an effective invention of the operations of this crossing. The figures of the Keeper, the Fictioneer, the Eraser of gods, and the Watchman materializing the novel project of a "metaphysics without metaphysics". These four poets who "passed", as Pessoa writes, "immaterially through his soul" contain an unheard of affirmative power: beyond the shattered core of metaphysics, they poetically bear a renewed thinking of being.

This book is dedicated
to Armand Guibert,
the Intercessor.

Judith Balso has taught seminars on Fernando Pessoa, Wallace Stevens, Pier Paolo Pasolini, Osip Mandelstam, and Dante at the Collège International de Philosophie in Paris, France. She currently teaches poetry and philosophy at the European Graduate School in Saas-Fee, Switzerland. Her latest book, *Affirmation de la poésie* is published by NOUS editions, France.

# Bibliography

Note from Judith Balso

I am the author of the (French) translations of the excerpts of poems (and prose) by Pessoa contained in this book, at least for those which can be found in the public domain. Conversely, what was not found within the public domain has not been re-translated. This was not by choice, but for completely extrinsic reasons related to the current rights of citation. My own preference would have been to use for the most part the translations of Armand Guibert, who I would like to thank for his pioneering and innovative work. We owe him gratitude for bringing this poet to France.

*

The Portuguese editions of Pessoa's oeuvre and that of his heteronyms consulted in the construction of this book are the following:

*Obra poética*, single volume, selection, organization and notes by Maria Aliete Galhoz, Rio de Janeiro, Editora Nova Aguilar, 1983.

*Obras de Fernando Pessoa*, 3 vol., introduction, organisation, bibliography, and notes by Antonio Quadros and Dalila Pereira da Costa, Porto, Lello & Irmão Editores, 1986.

*Edição crítica de Fernando Pessoa,* Lisbonne, Imprensa Nacional-Casa da Moeda, t. II, *Poemas de Álvaro de Campos,* 1990 ; t. III, *Poemas de Ricardo Reis,* 1994.

*Livro do Desassossego por Bernardo Soares,* choice and transcription of the texts by Maria Aliete Galhoz and Teresa Sobral Cunha, Lisbonne, Edições Atica, 1982.

*Livro do Desassossego por Bernardo Soares,* 1st and 2nd parts, introduction and new organization of texts by Antonio Quadros, Livros de bolso Europa-America, 1986.

*Mensagem,* photographs by Jorge Barros, Porto, Edições Asa, 1988.

*O manuscrito de O guardador de rebanhos de Alberto Caeiro,* éd. fac-similé, presentation and critical text by Ivo Castro, Lisbon, Publições Dom Quixote, 1986.

*Orfeu 3,* preparation of text, introduction and chronology by Arnaldo Saraiva, Lisbon, Edições Atica, 1984.

Lopes, Teresa Rita, *Pessoa por conhecer,* t. I, *Roteiro para uma expedição*; t. II, *Textos para um novo mapa,* Lisbon, Editorial Estampa, 1990.

Blanco, José, *Fernando Pessoa, esboço de uma bibliografia,* Lisbon, Imprensa Nacional-Casa da Moeda-Centro de Estudos Pessoanos, 1983.

*

The French versions of Pessoa and his heteronyms consulted in the construction of this book are the following:

The translations of Armand Guibert:

*Bureau de tabac et autres poèmes,* Paris, Caractères, 1955.

*Fernando Pessoa,* by Armand Guibert, Paris, Seghers, coll. "Poètes d'aujourd'hui", 1975.

*Fernando Pessoa, Visage avec masques*, Lausanne, Alfred Eibel, 1978.

*Ode Maritime* [Álvaro de Campos], Saint-Clément-la-Rivière, Fata Morgana, 1980.

*Opium à bord, poème* d'*Álvaro de Campos*, Le Muy, Éd. Unes. 1987.

*Poésies d'Álvaro de Campos*, with Le Gardeur de troupeaux et les autres poemes d'Alberto Caeiro, Paris, Gallimard, coll. "Poésie", 1987.


The collegial translations from Christian Bourgois :

*Cancioneiro*, poems, 1911-1935, trans. Fr. By Michel Chandeigne and Patrick Quillier, in collaboration with Maria Antonia Câmara Manuel and Liberto Cruz, with the participation of Lucien Kebren and Maria Teresa Leitão, and a preface by Robert Bréchon, Paris, Christian Bourgois, 1988.

*Oeuvres poetiques d'Álvaro de Campos*, trans. Fr. by Michel Chandeigne and Pierre Léglise-Costa, with the participation of René Tavernier and a preface by Armand Guibet, 1988.

*Poèmes d'Álvaro de Campos*, new edition., trans. Fr. by Patrick Quillier, with the participation of Maria Antonia Câmara Manuel, 2001.

*Poèmes ésotériques, Message, Le Marin*, trans. Fr. by Michel Chandeigne and Patrick Quillier, in collaboration with Maria Antonia Câmara Manuel and Françoise Laye, with the participation of Fernando Antunes, 1988.

*Poèmes païennes d'Alberto Caeiro et Ricardo Reis*, trans. Fr. By Michel Chandeigne, Patrick Quillier and Maria Antonia Câmara Manuel, 1989.

From Éditions de la Différence :

*Ode maritime* (et autres poemes d'Álvaro de Campos), trans. Fr. by Dominique Touati et Michel Chandeigne, collection "Orphée", 1990.

*Œuvres completes de Fernando Pessoa,* t. III, *Poesies et prose d'Álvaro de Campos,* trans. Fr. by Dominique Touati and Simone Biberfeld, 1989.

*Œuvres complètes de Fernando Pessoa,* t. IV, *Poèmes de Alberto Caeiro,* trans. Fr. by Dominique Touati, 1989.


From Éditions Unes :

*Bureau de tabac,* new trans. Fr. by Rémy Hourcade, 1988.

*Le Gardeur de troupeaux, poème d'Alberto Caeiro,* trans. Fr. by Rémy Hourcade and Jean Louis Giovannoni, 1986.

*Message,* éd. bilingue and trans. Fr. By Bernard Sesé, Paris, José Corti/Unesco, 1988.

*

The French versions of *The Book of Disquiet* consulted in the construction of this book are the following:

*Le livre de l'intranquillité de Bernardo Soares,* 3 vol., trans. Fr. by Françoise Laye, Paris, Christian Bourgois, 1992.

*Le livre de l'intranquillité de Bernardo Soares,* 3 vol., trans. Fr. by Françoise Laye, new edition, corrected and reviewed, Paris, Christian Bourgois, 1999.

*Le livre de l'inquiétude par Bernardo Soares,* translated fragments by Inès Oseki-Dépré, Le Muy, Éd. Unes, 1987.

The English versions of the Book of Disquiet consulted for the construction of this book are the following :

*The Book of Disquiet*, Fernando Pessoa, trans. Richard Zenith, Penguin Classics, 2002.

*The Keeper of Sheep*, Fernando Pessoa, bilingual edition, trans. Edwin Honig and Susan M. Brown, Sheep Meadow, 1997.

*Poems of Fernando Pessoa,* Fernando Pessoa, trans. Edwin Honig, City Lights Publishers, 2001.

*Walt Whitman and The World,* Ed. By Gay Wilson and Ed Wilson, Iowa City, University of Iowa Press, 1995.

Lightning Source UK Ltd.
Milton Keynes UK
UKOW04f1208230215

246741UK00001B/465/P